Money Miracles

A Proven System to Attract Money and the Things it Buys

by Kerry C. O'Hallaron (with Wallace D. Wattles)

**Thank you for purchasing this book.
Please review it on Amazon,
Goodreads, or the site of your choice so
we can make future editions even
better!**

Contents

Author's Foreword

"Money Miracles."

Catchy title, isn't it? But who is the author, and why should you read this book?

If you asked me to answer why you should read it in just two words, they would be, "It works!" If you allowed me three words, they would be, "This stuff works!" If you were really generous and allowed me four words, they would be, "Because it really works!" You get the point.

How do I know this?

You will not see my name on the list of the world's wealthiest people in Forbes Magazine. I like it that way, but I still do pretty well. Way more than 99% of the people on this planet would see me as *rich*. However, this book is about the science of attracting money, a skill which you can easily use on your personal mission to build wealth, improve the world, or whatever else you wish to do. It was really a burning desire to learn and to share how ordinary people seem to have all the "luck," at least when it comes to money and the things it buys, that resulted in this book being published.

For many of my earlier years, it was my goal to become *rich*. During those years, I did *not* live in poverty. I do not have one of those "rags to riches" stories (and you'll read later on in this book why I wouldn't tell such a story even if I did). I always had plenty – a nice roof over my head, decent transportation, more than enough food for my family – I just wasn't *rich* and I wasn't getting *rich*.

I tried every plan, scheme, business, and program you could possibly think of. I followed every guru there was. They all got richer because of the things I bought from them, and I continued to live a nice and comfortable life, but not a wealthy life.

Only within the last ten years have I come to understand a new way of thinking about money and the things it buys. I started learning from people who were focused not on the exact method of making money, but on the *process* that causes one person to attract money and another to stay broke. I stopped worrying about such things as highly leveraged real estate, trading stock options, and a myriad of available business opportunities; and focused on the understanding the attraction process itself.

And it started working in a way that almost seemed formulaic. I said to myself, "I did this, this, and this; and then money came to me. I bet I could repeat that." I repeated it and it worked!

I have followed many of the great teachers of this process. They all have pretty much the same message, just with different words. Curiously, I began working backwards to see where each of them got their inspiration. Invariably, the roads led to my co-author, Wallace Wattles.

Let me explain. In 1910, Wattles wrote what many believe is a timeless classic entitled *The Science of Getting Rich*. I read it (in 2014, not in 1910) with a skeptical mind. The writing was beyond hopelessly outdated. However, every bit of the material somehow sounded familiar, even though I'd never heard of the book before, much less read it.

You see, as something of a "self-improvement junkie," I have listened to or read material from just about every motivational writer and speaker in existence over the last thirty years. As it turns out, every single one of them used one or more of the ideas from Wattles' book - they just changed the words to make them more appropriate for the times. So when I read Wattles' book, it gave me a gigantic sense of *déjà vu*, almost every time I turned a page! I felt like I'd heard this stuff before *because I had heard it before* - from every great and not-so-great name in motivational speaking and writing.

I'd learned that Wattles was the original source of much of the modern material on attracting money. And in recent years, I had the opportunity to determine which parts of that material actually work and which do not.

So, I teamed up with Wattles (in a manner of speaking, as he is no longer with us in the flesh) to write this book. Using his original text *The Science of Getting Rich* as my foundation, I modified the theme and completely re-wrote the material in the language of the twenty-first century, focusing on the parts that I've been able to prove and leaving out the things that were suspect.

How do I know this stuff works today? Because I've used it over the years on a daily basis, to attract a really decent income, a great life style, and more *stuff* than a person could possibly ask for. Wattles was simply kind enough to provide a foundation for me to articulate to you how I did it, how I continue to do it every day, and how you can do it too.

I hope you enjoy the miracles you are about to create. If you want to begin to actually create your own financial results, then you have your compelling reason for reading this book.

This stuff works!

Kerry C. O'Hallaron

Co-Author's Foreword

(Due to the fact that Mr. Wattles, now long deceased, could not be present for this writing, I have taken the liberty of writing his foreword for him in the first person, as if he were speaking the words himself. I'm pretty sure he would approve. - Kerry O'Hallaron)

My Dear Sirs:

I have not had the privilege of meeting the author, Kerry O'Hallaron. In my original text, The Science of Getting Rich, I counsel against bothering the deceased, even if they may be accessible on some earthly plane. Mr. O'Hallaron has kindly honored that request, and has not attempted to contact me. He has, however, made available to me a copy of his text, including his own foreword, and I wish to comment upon these.

Firstly, in his foreword, the author states that the language used in my original text was "beyond hopelessly outdated." I must respectfully take serious exception to that description. The language of my time was precise and well-ordered. It is you of the twenty-first century who have made such changes to our well-structured language as to "necessitate," in O'Hallaron's belief, the complete re-work of my original tome.

Secondly, I must point out what may be obvious: The titles of our two works bear more than subtle differences. I laid out an exact scientific process of joining the financially elite; ergo the title, <u>The Science of Getting Rich</u>. O'Hallaron, on the other hand, focuses on a process of attracting money. While that is indeed a step in the science of getting rich, it would seem to extend his version of my teachings to a great many more people than I did. Certainly, the principles I teach can be used by anyone, but it was truly expected that only a few would adopt them. So I must commend this author for writing a book that can assist anyone who wants to improve his financial position, and not simply those few who wish to begin approaching, as you call them "the 1%."

While neither the words nor the title of this book bear much resemblance to mine, the fundamentals are strikingly similar. O'Hallaron takes great care to teach of a connectivity which we all share, from which all abundance flows and into which we must tap if we are to gain additional resources. At the same time, he is cautious to not require the reader to adopt any particular spiritual belief set. Indeed, he effectively conveys that most of your modern religions, which are the same as were available during my time, are truly compatible with his teachings. His portrayal of the spiritual component of this teaching, while at the same time not imposing religion on the reader, is indeed artful.

O'Hallaron seemed to pay me a bit of a backhanded compliment by calling my original work a "timeless classic." I say this because he followed his statement by proceeding to change the title, the theme to some extent, and virtually every word of my work to fit your so-called "modern" times. "Timeless classic indeed," I thought. I must admit I was taken aback by all this, at first. If my work were indeed a timeless classic, then who is this individual to presume that he can improve upon it?

Upon review of his work, though, it has been demonstrated to me that he has a deep understanding of the application of these concepts, and is uniquely qualified to bring them to you in his own words and his own theme.

I therefore grant my wholehearted endorsement and seal of approval to this work, and encourage the reader to give it his fullest attention to the extent that you desire to scientifically improve your financial lot in life.

For Wallace D. Wattles, by Kerry C. O'Hallaron

Chapter 1
Yes, You DO Have a Right to be Rich

"Money isn't everything, but it ranks right up there with oxygen."

(Zig Ziglar, American author and speaker, 1926-2012)

It's just not right to say anything bad about poor people - including people who make a spiritual or personal choice to be poor. However, if you want to live a complete and successful life, it's really hard to do it without some level of wealth. It's hard, maybe impossible, for you or anyone else to rise to great heights in talent and personal development without a fair amount of money.

There's a reason for this. To develop your talents, you must have *things* (both tangible and intangible). You can't have *things* without the *money* to buy them! You need *things* to develop in mind, spirit, and body. It's simply the nature of our society that you need money to have things.

In this book, you and I will speak of a science of attracting money, or of creating "money miracles." You can take these terms literally, or you can interpret them as metaphors for getting rich, gaining great wealth, becoming financially sound - however you choose to view it.

In any case, the science of attracting money, or creating "money miracles," is essentially the basis for all advancement of humankind. The objective of our lives should be to develop, not just to stagnate. We are born with the right to all the development that we are capable of gaining.

Our right to life means our right to have free and unrestricted use of all the things which we might need for full mental, spiritual, and physical development - in other words, our right to attract money!

I'm not going to figuratively talk to you about wealth. Attracting money does not mean, at least to me, attracting just a little bit of money! Nobody should be satisfied with just a little, if he or she is capable of having, enjoying, and sharing more. (By the way, this book has no gender. Sometimes we will use the male gender; sometimes the female. Know that in all cases, we mean both.)

Nature serves the purpose of advancing and developing all life. Every person, including you and me, should have everything that helps to contribute to the power, elegance, beauty, and richness of life. In a sense, being content with anything less is sinful!

So how much money are we talking about here? In my opinion, if you have everything you want for living all of the life that you are capable of living, then that's how much we are talking about. That doesn't exactly put a dollar (or other currency) figure on it. But clearly, at a minimum, you need to have plenty of money to have everything you want.

We've advanced quite a bit as a civilization. Life has become very complex - not to the point of being rocket science, but complex regardless. If you want to live a complete life, it's going to require a chunk of change!

Our desire to become everything we can become is instinctive. It's human nature. We can't help wanting to be all that we can be. If you want to be successful in life, you can't do it without developing your full potential. To do that, you need things. To have things, you need money.

To paraphrase Zig Ziglar, the famous motivational speaker, money is about as essential to life as oxygen! So, understanding the science of attracting money is about one of the most important lessons you can learn in this life.

In spite of what some of us have been taught, there's nothing inherently wrong with wanting to attract money. If you want wealth, what you really want is a fuller, more abundant life. Having that desire is noble and praiseworthy, not wrong.

In fact, if you *don't* want to have enough money to buy everything you want, *that* is abnormal.

Consider these three things that we all live for:

1. Our bodies
2. Our minds
3. Our spirits (or souls)

(Note: What I am teaching you in this book applies regardless of your spiritual beliefs. The word *spirit* may have a deeply religious meaning to you. Or, it may mean something more secular, such as an unexplained connectivity that we all seem to have. Please use references to such concepts as *spirit*, *God*, etc. as appropriate to your own beliefs.)

None of these three is any more important or more *sacred* than the other. They're all important. None of them can fully develop unless the other two are also fully developed. It's inappropriate for you to live only for the spirit while neglecting your mind and body. It's not right to live only for your mind, and to neglect the body or spirit.

You and I have both seen what happens when people live just for the body and neglect the mind and spirit - sooner or later, all three disappear.

We've all seen that real life means being all you can be in body, mind, and spirit. People will try to convince you otherwise, but nobody can be truly happy or satisfied unless his/her body is living a full life.

The same is true of the mind and spirit. Wherever there is unfulfilled potential, there is unsatisfied desire.

You just can't live your fullest life without good food, comfortable clothes, warm shelter - and without working yourself to death to gain these things. You also need both rest and fun, for your physical well-being.

Your mind can't fully develop without reading, learning, travel, observation, and sharing your brain power with others. Just like the body, your mind also needs its own form of *fun*. You can get this by surrounding yourself with all the objects of art and beauty that you are capable of using and appreciating.

If you want to live fully in spirit, you must have love. This can take the form of a spouse, a significant other, family - or just people that you care deeply for. It's difficult to fully express love when you're poor. People take great pleasure in giving gifts and intangible things to those who they love. You can express love naturally and spontaneously through giving. If you have nothing to give, it's difficult do your best as a husband or wife, father or mother, citizen, or person.

To have the best life for your body, you need material things - not to excess, but you do need them. The same applies to developing your mind and spirit.

The only conclusion you can then draw is that it's *important* to attract money if you want to have a full life. It's normal and perfectly okay, to *want* to attract money. If you are a normal man or woman, then it's hard to feel otherwise.

So if it's normal and okay to *want* to attract money, then it's normal and okay to study the *science* of attracting money, which is what we teach you in this book. Consider this: If you *don't* study the science of attracting money, you are neglecting your duties to yourself, your God, and humanity. You owe it to your God and to humanity to make the most of yourself - and that includes understanding the science of attracting money.

Are you getting this? It's science, but it's not rocket science. Let's have some fun while we learn how it all works!

Chapter 2
Attracting Money is a Science (Just Not *Rocket* Science)

"I've been rich, and I've been poor. Rich is better."

(Beatrice Kaufman, American producer, editor, and publisher, 1895-1945)

Attracting money really isn't rocket science. I say that because it simply requires a formula that I'm giving to you right here and now in this book. I use it daily. It works. You can use it and you can share it.

That said, there is still a *science* to attracting money. It is an exact science, just like algebra or arithmetic. You must follow certain laws which govern the process. Though once you learn and obey them, it is almost guaranteed that you will attract money.

There is a certain way you need to act in order to begin attracting money and the things it buys. If you do things in that *certain way,* whether accidentally or deliberately, you will attract money. If you don't do things in that *certain way*, no matter what your talents are or how hard you work, you are going to stay broke!

Can we talk about natural laws? One of my favorites is that, "like attracts like." Said a bit more eloquently, "like causes always produce like effects." What this means to you, as we'll discuss throughout this book, is that if you think it, there's a very good possibility you can cause its physical equivalent to appear in your life.

Let me prove this concept to you, in relation to attracting money.

Attracting money is not environmental. If it were, everyone in every nice middle class neighborhood would become wealthy. The people of one city would all be wealthy, while the people in other towns would all be poor. The residents of one state would all be rolling in dough, while those in the state next door would all be dirt poor. (The key word here is *all*. We do see trends in neighborhoods, cities, and states - but it's not the neighborhood, city, or state that causes financial growth.)

You don't have to look far to find rich and poor living near each other, often in the same neighborhoods, cities, and towns; and often working in the same professions. When two people are in the same town and in the same business, and one gets rich while the other remains broke, it shows that attracting money is not *primarily* a matter of environment.

Some environments may be more favorable than others. However, when there are two people in the same business and the same neighborhood, and one gets rich while the other one stays broke, it shows that attracting money is the result of doing things a certain way.

Also, if you have the ability to do things in this certain way, you don't have it solely as a result of talent. Many people who are exceptionally talented stay poor. Many others who don't really have much talent get rich. Not only is this stuff not rocket science - it's not *fair*, either.

I've made a life of studying people who have gotten rich. I've learned that they are typically very average people - who have attracted a lot of money! Generally, they don't have talent that matches their wealth.

For example, consider Bill Gates, the founder of Microsoft. Sure, he was knowledgeable of software development at a time when the desktop PC was ready to come of age - but so were many others in his time. Gates grew to become one of the wealthiest people in the world. People who knew him "back when" would argue that his software development talent was only adequate. So how did he get so wealthy?

I suggest to you that people do not attract

money because they have talents and abilities that you don't have. They generally attract money because they happen to do things in a certain way. They don't get there by saving or by being thrifty (although this is still a good quality to have). Many very thrifty people are still broke, while many free spenders manage to get rich.

Attracting money is also not the result of doing things which others fail to do. Two people in the same profession often do almost the exact same things and one gets rich while the other stays broke or becomes bankrupt. Consider your own profession - do you know someone who does exactly what you've done, yet they've done much better (or worse) than you financially?

There's really only one conclusion - if you want to attract money, you have to do things a *certain* way! You'll hear me referencing that *certain way* throughout this book, and explaining it a bit down the line. From this point forward, we'll refer to it as *The Money Miracle Way*.

Now, if attracting money is the result of doing things *The Money Miracle Way*, and if like causes always produce like effects, then what can you do with this information? You, and anyone else who does things in that way, can attract money! Even though it's not rocket science, it is definitely scientific.

"So," you ask, "is *The Money Miracle Way* so difficult that only a few can follow it?"

Fair question. The answer is no. As I've explained above, it doesn't apply to natural ability. Talented people get rich. Blockheads get rich. Brilliant people get rich. Stupid people get rich. Physically strong people get rich. Weak and sickly people get rich. Of course, it's essential that you have some degree of ability to think and understand. But if you have enough sense to read and understand what I'm teaching you, you have all the natural ability you need to attract money.

If attracting money is the result of doing things *The Money Miracle Way,* and if like causes always produce like effects, then any human alive who can do things *The Money Miracle Way* can attract money. This whole thing becomes a matter of exact science.

I've also shown you that attracting money is not a matter of environment. Sure, your location counts for something. It's probably not a good idea to go to the middle of the Sahara Desert to open a business. Also, it's definitely essential that you deal with people if you want to attract money. It's best to be where the people are, or where they are accessible. It's also best to be near (or accessible to) people who *want* to do business with you.

But that's about it as far as environment goes.

If anyone else in your neighborhood, city, state, or country can attract money, so can you!

As I've mentioned, it's also not a matter of choosing the right business or career. People attract money in every business and in every career. At the same time, their next-door neighbors in the same career may stay broke. Of course, you will do best in a business that you like and that will not wear you out. If you have certain well developed talents or skills, you'll do best in the career or business that can use those skills.

You'll also do best in a business that fits your locality. Don't open a snow ski resort in Florida. Don't open an ice cream store in Greenland (but do consider Florida). Consider a salmon fishing business in the Pacific Northwest of the U.S., but not in Florida (where there are no salmon).

But other than these obvious limitations, you don't have to be in a particular business to attract money. You just have to learn to do things *The Money Miracle Way.* If you are in business now, and everyone else in your area is getting rich in the same business, you can too. If you aren't, it's because you are not doing things *The Money Miracle Way* and the other folks are.

Lack of money doesn't necessarily stop you from getting rich, either. We've all heard the old saying, "You've got to have money to make money." For many, though, that's just an excuse.

Sure, as you get more capital, it becomes easier to expand more quickly. But if you *have* said capital, you're already rich and you don't need to figure out how to become rich!

No matter how poor you may be, if you begin to do things *The Money Miracle Way,* you will begin to attract money (honestly - it works!). You will also begin to have working capital. Gaining capital is part of the process. It's also part of the result you are guaranteed to get once you start doing things *The Money Miracle Way.*

You may be the poorest man on the continent and be deeply in debt. You may not have much in the way of friends, influence, or resources. I'm pretty sure all of the above applied to Donald Trump when he went bankrupt not too many years ago - yet look at him today.

However, if you begin to do things *The Money Miracle Way,* you have no choice but to begin attracting money. Like causes produce like effects for you, me, and everyone else.

If you don't have capital, you can get capital. If you are in the wrong business, you can get into the right business. If you are in the wrong location, you can move to the right location.

The key is to start operating *The Money Miracle Way* in your present job or business, and in your present location, so that you can begin to see that this stuff actually works.

Chapter 3
But Is There Enough Opportunity to Go Around?

"It's simple arithmetic: "Your income can grow only to the extent you do."

T. Harv Eker, Canadian-American author and trainer, 1954-)

I want you to ask you to remember two important ideas:

A) "Broke" is a state of mind

B) "Broke" is, by its nature, temporary

Now, put these two thoughts together, and "broke" becomes nothing more than a temporary state of mind!

Have you ever had a major financial setback? A big opportunity taken away? I certainly have. But remember this: Nobody is *kept* broke because of an opportunity that has been taken away. Nobody is *kept* broke because other people have monopolized all the wealth and put a fence around it.

You may be kept out of certain types of

business. However, there are always other options. As an example, it might be difficult for you to gain control of one of the world's largest banks or one of the world's largest auto manufacturers. Those ships have already left port, so to speak.

However, there are plenty of businesses in their infancy. As an example, here is one: alternative energy. I'm not an expert in the use of solar power but I'll bet you'll be seeing incredible growth in solar electricity, solar water heating, etc. (In fact, my good friend A.J. O'Brien has a short but important book on this subject called *Free Electricity Forever*. Check it out at Amazon and tell him Kerry sent you.)

If you are working in a well-established field such as banking, you may do well but you may not ever own the bank. However, if you begin acting *The Money Miracle Way,* you may soon find yourself leaving that field. Who knows what you will end up doing?

You might start a solar contracting business. You might own a fish farm to supply high quality, low cost food. You might find some way to provide a valuable service to others as a consultant, using today's advanced communications and information technology to leverage your operation. Whatever you do, please do not say that it's impossible to get the money to finance one of these ventures. I'm going to prove to you that it's not impossible, and that you can absolutely get capital and whatever else you need if you operate *The Money Miracle Way.*

Consider this: Opportunity flows in a number of different directions, according to the needs of the world as a whole. This is also affected by the stage of social evolution in which we find ourselves.

For example, a hundred years ago, the trend in the United States and many developed nations was towards agriculture and manufacturing. Today, of course, that tide has shifted in many places toward things like electronics, telecommunications, and service industries. If you're willing to go with the tide rather than against it, there is plenty of opportunity.

So today, if you are working in a potentially *dying* industry (such as newspaper publishing, for example), that does not mean there is no opportunity available to you. You and others in such industries are not being kept down by *the man.* You are not being stymied by the big money interests. As a class, the folks working in dying industries are where they are (and hopefully you are not one of them) because they do not do things *The Money Miracle Way.*

If the workers in dying industries chose to do so, they could follow the examples of their brothers in emerging industries (solar power, wind power, and bio-tech, just to name a few), and develop successful businesses within those classes. And not to get political on you but if the same workers really wanted to, they could elect people from the working class to office and get laws passed that favored the development of such emerging industries. In a few years, they could *own* those fields. (You don't have to read too far into modern history to see this happening in the aftermath of World War II, in some of the countries which were less than successful in the war itself.)

You see, sooner or later, the worker bees can and will shift to become the ruling class - once they do things *The Money Miracle Way*. The law of wealth is exactly the same for them as it is for everyone else. They just have to learn this, but they will stay where they are until they do learn it.

However, an individual such as you does not need to be held down (and should not be held down) by the ignorance or the laziness of the rest of the group. All you have to do is follow the tide of opportunity. I'll tell you how to do that in this book.

Let's be clear - there are plenty of resources to go around. Nobody is kept in poverty by a shortage in the supply of money. There is more than enough of that for everybody.

There is enough building material in the

United States alone to build a home the size of the U.S. Capitol building for every family on the planet! The United States, with a little effort, could produce enough natural and artificial fabric to clothe every person in the world in their finest "Sunday best." Just in the United States alone, there is enough food to feed every person on the planet in style.

The *visible* supply of these resources is practically limitless, and the *invisible* supply really is limitless. Consider this theory: Everything you see on earth is made from one thing we'll call the *original substance* (you can think of it as "energy" if you wish).

Everything flows from the original substance. New forms (new things) are constantly being made but all of them can be traced back to the original substance.

Now, I know this is getting a little heavy but follow along with me. There is no limit to the supply of original substance (which, again, you can refer to as "energy" if you prefer). The universe is made of it but it wasn't all used up in the making of the universe.

Everywhere you look, in every nook and cranny, every bit of empty space is permeated and filled with the original substance, with the formless stuff, with this raw material of all things. As much of it already exists, there may still be ten thousand times more available. Even if we used up that much, we still would not exhaust the supply.

The point is, nobody, *nobody*, is poor because nature is poor or because there is not enough to go around. That's just not the case. Nature has all the riches that all of us need. The supply will never run short.

This stuff we're calling original substance is alive with creative energy (an interesting thought - can "energy" be alive with energy?) It is constantly producing more forms. When the supply of building material is exhausted, we'll come up with new forms of building materials. When oil starts to run dry, we'll come up with new energy sources.

When the soil is depleted to the point that we can't grow food on it, we'll figure out how to renew it or we'll figure out other sources of food. When all of the gold and silver has been dug out of the ground; if we still need it, we'll figure out how to get more or how to get alternatives. This is not just a bunch of untested theory - it has always been this way.

Whatever our needs are, this formless stuff responds to them. If mankind needs something, formless stuff (which you might even more simply think of as "the universe") will produce it.

Perhaps you've noticed that we've moved a bit into the metaphysical here. If you have a religious belief set, I hope you'll find these concepts absolutely compatible with your beliefs. If, for some reason, they are incompatible, please read them with an open mind. It may only take a bit of re-framing to synchronize them with your religious or spiritual belief set.

So, what we said above about the universe responding to needs is *collectively* true of mankind, not necessarily of each member of the human race. The race, as a whole, is always filthy rich. To the extent that individuals (hopefully not you) are broke, it is because they don't follow *The Money Miracle Way* of doing things that causes the individual to attract money.

In a manner of speaking, the universe is intelligent. It "thinks." It is alive, always moving towards more life. Life has a natural and inherent impulse to seek to live more. Intelligence tends, by its nature, to enlarge itself; to try to extend its boundaries and find fuller expression. All of the things, living and non-living, have been made by the universe; throwing itself into form in order to express itself more fully.

The universe is a great living presence, always moving inherently toward more life and fuller functioning. The whole purpose of nature is to advance life. That's its driving motive. That is why everything which can support life is plentiful. It's theoretically impossible for the world, as a whole, to be lacking in resources. Again, that can happen to an individual but not to the whole.

If you're broke, you are not kept that way by a lack of supply. The resources are there. You can tap into them in limitless fashion if you'll just do it *The Money Miracle Way.*

You've managed to get through some pretty heavy philosophy in this chapter. There's a little more to come, and then we start getting down to the "meat."

Chapter 4
Ready to Go? Start Here!

"Thoughts become things."

(Bob Proctor, Canadian author, 1935 -)

I hope you read this whole book cover to cover more than once. However, if you only remember one concept from the entire book, remember this one:

The only thing which can attract money and the things it buys, is *thought*.

Thought. That's it! Spoiler alert - the rest of the material in this book is critically important but when you are done, you'll be able to trace it all back to this one sentence.

Now, let's talk a little more metaphysical theory here. All things are made from, flow from, come from, a *substance* which thinks. A thought in this substance can actually produce the thing that is being thought of (whether you or someone else is thinking the thought).

The universe moves according to its

thoughts. Every form, every process that you see in nature is a visible expression of a thought in the universe. As the universe thinks of a form, that form becomes real. As it thinks of a motion, that motion occurs. If you can get your head around these concepts, then you understand how things have been *manifested* throughout history.

We live in a thought world, which is part of a thought universe. The universe takes the form of its thought, and moves according to it.

I know this is some very heavy philosophy but it's designed to get you thinking about *thinking*.

So, holding the idea of a circling system of suns and worlds, the universe takes the form of these bodies and moves them as it thinks. Thinking the form of a slow-growing oak tree, it moves accordingly and produces the tree, though it may take a hundred years to complete the job.

In creating or manifesting, the universe seems to move down the path it has created. The thought of an oak tree does not cause an instant, full-grown tree. However, it does start the forces in motion which will ultimately produce the tree.

As with the oak tree, every thought of *form* (in other words, not just an idea but something tangible), impressed on the universe, ultimately results in the creation of that form but always, or almost always, along the predetermined growth and action path.

So, as an example, imagine someone planning to build a "McMansion." They sufficiently impress the thought of that house on the universe, you hear a *poof*, and the McMansion appears. Not! It doesn't work that way.

However, that thought would cause the creative energies already working in business and finance to be more focused on the prompt design and completion of the McMansion. If those channels did not exist, the McMansion might be built even more quickly rather than more slowly, because there may be fewer hoops to be cleared in the process.

What I'm trying to teach you is this: If you can properly impress any thought of form onto the universe, the form you are thinking of will ultimately result. That's a pretty powerful statement, isn't it? Think, and it shall become.

People are thinking machines. They can originate thought. Whatever forms that a person can fashion with her hands must first exist in thought. She cannot shape anything until she has first thought that thing.

Up to this point, people have largely

confined their efforts to the work of their hands. They've used manual labor with the help of tools and machines, trying to modify or change forms that already exist. Thus far, most people really have not though much about trying to create new forms by impressing those thoughts upon the universe. (Of course, those who know *The Money Miracle Way* actually do exactly that!)

When you envision a form through thought, you take (in your mind) material from nature to make an image of the form. At this point, though, you have made little or no effort to cooperate with the universe. You may not have yet dreamed that you can actually have what you have envisioned.

In the ordinary course of events, people reshape and modify existing forms all the time through manual (and machine) labor. Most people, though, have given little thought to the question of whether they can produce things from the universe by communicating their thoughts to it. I propose to prove that this is possible; that any person (including you) can do it. I also propose to show you *how*.

As my first step, please consider the following fundamental propositions.

First, I suggest that there is one original substance, which I will call *formless stuff*, from which all things are made. We've learned in school that there are many elements. I'm suggesting they are all different presentations of the same element. Everything, whether organic or inorganic, is nothing but a different shape of the same stuff.

Further, this stuff is thinking stuff. A thought held within it produces the form of that thought. Thought, when impressed on or held in the universe, produces shapes. People are thinking "centers," capable of original thought. (Not all of us use that capability as much as we should, but that's entirely another issue.) So, if a person can communicate his thought to the universe, he can, in a sense, create or form the very thing that he thinks about.

Are you getting this? Perhaps you've heard of the notion that *thought creates your reality*. Maybe you understood that to mean that thought creates your *perception* of reality. What I am telling you is that thought can ultimately create the things around you which represent your reality!

To say it another way, there is a thinking stuff from which all things are made. In its original state, this thinking stuff permeates, penetrates, and fills the nooks and crannies of the universe. A thought in this stuff produces the thing that was the subject of the thought.

People, in other words, have the power to

create things with their thoughts. By impressing their thoughts upon the universe, they can cause the things they think about to be created.

Can I prove these crazy theories? I can and I will, with both logic and experience.

Working backwards from the phenomena of form and thought brings us to the idea that there is one original thinking substance. Then working forward from this thinking substance, we come to your power to cause the formation of the things you think about. I've done a lot of experimentation and found this logic to be absolutely true.

For me, personally, here is the strongest proof. If *one* person who reads this book attracts money by doing what the book tells her to do, that is evidence to support my claim. But if *every* person who does what the book tells him to do begins to attract money, that should be proof positive for everyone - at least until someone goes through the process and fails.

So the theory is true until the process fails - and I suggest to you that the process will not fail! Every person who does exactly what this book tells him/her to do will begin to attract money - including you!

As I've said, people attract money by doing things *The Money Miracle Way*. To be able to do things *The Money Miracle Way*, people need to learn to think *The Money Miracle Way*.

Your own way, or method of doing things, is the direct result of the way you *think* about things. If you want to be able to *do* things the way you *want* to do them, you have to learn to *think* the way you *want* to think. That is the first step to creating money miracles.

If you can think what you want to think, then you are thinking *truth*, regardless of appearances. Every person has within him/her the natural and inherent power to think what he wants to think - it's just hard work to actually do it! It's harder to think what you want to think than to think what the appearance of things suggests you should think (that is, thinking according to appearances).

Thinking according to appearances is easy. Thinking *truth*, regardless of appearances, is very difficult - possibly the hardest work a person can perform. People are quick to avoid the hard work of sustained and consecutive thought - it may be the hardest job in the world!

This is especially true when truth is something other than the way things seem to be. Everything in the physical world elicits a corresponding thought in the mind of the observer. If that thought is inconsistent with truth, then the observer can only change it by consistently holding the thought of truth.

As an example, if you look at someone with a terrible disease, that will produce the "form" of disease in your own mind. Ultimately, if you don't take the care to replace that form with reality (truth), you will end up with disease in your own body. (*Do not* try this at home; it is actually true. It may or may not happen overnight - but rest assured, it will happen.) The truth that you need to replace that form with is that there is no disease *per se;* it is only an appearance and the reality is health.

As another example, if you see signs of poverty, they will produce corresponding "forms" of poverty in your own mind. You need to replace that with the truth that there is no poverty; there is only abundance. (Be particularly careful here. *Of course* there are people who are desperately lacking in their share of the abundance that is out there. We'll talk later about how to help them, if you wish. But be careful to avoid dwelling on the negative, such as the conditions in which those folks live. Remember that thought ultimately creates things.)

To think health when you are surrounded by the appearance of disease, or to think riches when you are in the middle of the appearance of poverty, requires a great deal of mind power. But once you acquire this power, you become a *master mind*. You can, in a sense, conquer fate. You can have what you want. But you can only get this power if you accept a basic fact that lies beyond appearances. That fact is that there is one thinking substance, from which and by which all things are made.

Once you get this, then you need to grasp the truth that every thought held in this substance becomes a form; and people can impress their thoughts on the substance in such a way that they take form and become visible things. When you realize this, you will lose all doubt and fear, because you know you can create what you want to create. You can get what you want to have. You can become what you want to be.

As a first step to attracting money, you must believe the three fundamentals that I've laid out in this chapter. Here they are again, for your ease of reference:

1. There is a thinking stuff from which all things are made and which, in its original state, permeates, penetrates, and fills every nook and cranny of the universe.
2. A thought, held in this substance, produces the thing that is imaged by the thought.
3. People can form things in their thoughts and, by impressing their thoughts upon formless substance (aka the universe),

*they can cause the things they think about
to be created.*

To close out this chapter, in order for this stuff to work, you must adopt it. You'll encounter other beliefs, teachings, and theories which are inconsistent. Inconsistencies will cause you to lose focus.

You need to dwell on this concept until it is fixed in your mind; until it has become your habitual thought. Read these statements over and over. Fix every word in your memory and meditate on them until you firmly believe what they are saying.

If a doubt crosses your mind, get rid of it as if it were a sin. Don't listen to arguments against these concepts. If your spiritual beliefs don't permit you to believe these principles, check again to see if there is room for adjustment of your beliefs. If your spiritual beliefs permit you to think in terms of creating money miracles, hopefully they also permit you to adopt what I'm teaching you.

Don't go to seminars or workshops that teach anything inconsistent with these principles. Don't read magazines or books which teach you something different. If you get mixed up in your beliefs and you are not sure what to believe, this stuff simply won't work.

Don't ask me (or anyone else) *why* this stuff is true. Don't speculate as to *how* it can be true. Simply accept it on faith. That's where it begins; that's the first step. Attracting money is not rocket science, but it is a science; and that science begins with your absolute acceptance of these principles on faith.

Chapter 5
What is a "Bigger" Life?

"All the resources we think we're running out of are really inventions of the human mind - and there is no limit to the human mind."

(Paul Zane Pilzer, American economist, 1954-)

Have you read a book called *God Wants You to Be Rich*? It's by an economist, Paul Zane Pilzer. It's billed as a "theology of economics." The essence of the book is that wealth, properly acquired and used, benefits mankind infinitely more than does poverty.

Of course, this concept is the opposite of what many religions teach. Often, they teach that wealth is bad, wealthy people are bad, and the pursuit of wealth is bad. Some even go as far as to teach, or imply, that poverty is somehow good.

If you want to attract money, though, you have to somehow shake such beliefs. You must get rid of that idea that God, or deity as you believe, wants you to be poor, and/ or is better served by you being poor.

The intelligent substance which *is* all, which

lives in all, and which lives in *you*, is a consciously living substance.

Being a consciously living substance, it inherently desires that every living intelligence, including you, increases in life. Every living thing must continually attempt to enlarge or increase its life; because life, by its very essence, must increase itself. When a seed drops to the ground, it springs into action. In the act of living, it produces a hundred more seeds. Life, just by living, multiplies itself. It must forever continue to become more, if it wants to continue being at all.

The same applies to intelligence. It has the same need for continuous growth or increase. Every time you think a thought, it makes it necessary for you to think another thought. Try thinking one thought without think the next one - it can't be done! Consciousness is continually expanding.

Every time you learn a fact, it leads you to learn yet another fact. Knowledge is continually increasing.

Every talent you cultivate causes you to want to cultivate another talent.

Life urges you to *know* more, to *do* more, and to *be* more. In order to know more, to do more, and to be more, you must *have* more. You must have things to use, because you learn and do and become only by using things. You *must* attract money, so that you can live more.

The desire for wealth is simply the tendency towards a larger life seeking its fulfillment. Every desire is an unexpressed possibility trying to come into action. Desire is caused by power which is not yet manifest. The thing that makes you want more money is the very same thing which makes a plant grow. It is life - seeking its fullest expression.

The one living substance is necessarily subject to this inherent law of all life. It is filled with the desire to live more. That is why it has the need to create things. The one substance would prefer to live more in you. Therefore, it wants you to have all the things you can use. It is God's desire that you should attract money. He wants you to attract money because He can express Himself better through you if you have plenty of things to use in giving Him that expression. He can live more in you if you have unlimited access to the things you need and want in life.

The universe wants you to have everything you want to have. Nature is happy with your plans. Nature, and everything in it, is in your favor. All you need to do is make up your mind that this is true.

It's critical, however, that your own purpose

must harmonize with the purpose that is in the universe. You must want all of life, a real life, and not just pleasure and gratification. Life is the performance of all of life's functions. You can only really live in harmony when you are performing every function - physical, mental, and spiritual - fully but not to excess.

You should not want to attract money to live like a pig, to live solely for the gratification of pleasure. That is not a real life. At the same time, though, every physical function is a part of life, and you can't live completely if you deny yourself the normal, healthy physical expression of earthly desires.

You should not want just to enjoy mental pleasures such as gaining knowledge, gratifying your ambitions, outshining others, or being famous. Each one of these is a legitimate part of life. However, if you live for the pleasures of the intellect alone, you will only have a partial life and you will never be satisfied with what you've got.

You should not want to attract money solely for the good of others, to lose yourself for the salvation of mankind, to experience the joys of philanthropy and sacrifice. These joys of the spirit are only a part of life. They are no better or no worse than any other part.

You might wish to attract money so that you can eat, drink, and have fun when it's time to do these things; so that you can fill your life with beautiful things, travel, feed your mind, and develop your intellect so that you can love people and do kind things; and be able to play a better part in helping the world find peace and truth. Be careful with the altruism part of that statement, though. Altruism is great, but *extreme* altruism is no better and no worse than extreme selfishness. They are both huge mistakes.

Get rid of the crazy idea that God wants you to completely sacrifice yourself for others and that you can win his favor by doing so. God simply does not require that of you. What He wants is that you make the most of yourself, for yourself and for others. You can help others more by making the most of yourself than in any other way. You can make the most of yourself only by attracting the money to buy the things you want and need, for whatever legitimate purposes you have. So, it's clearly not only right, but the best thing you can do - go give your best efforts to attracting money.

Remember, though, that the desire of substance is for all people, not just you, and its movements must be for more life for all people. You can't force it to work for less life for any other people because it is equally within everyone, seeking riches and life.

Intelligent substance will make things for you, but it will not take things away from someone else and give them to you. You should remember these guidelines:

- It's not about competition. Get rid of that thought.
- You need to *create,* not compete for the things that have already been created.
- You don't have to take anything from anyone. Don't even think about it.
- You don't have to make "win-lose" deals with anyone. That's a huge trap.
- You don't have to cheat or take advantage.
- You don't need to let anyone work for you for less than the job is actually worth.
- You don't have to *covet* the property of others. You don't even need to be envious of things others have that you wouldn't mind having. Nobody has anything that you couldn't have another one of (or something similar, or better), without you having to take it from the other person.

You are to become a creator, not a competitor. You are going to get what you want. But you are not going to get it at the expense of others. In fact, when you get what you want, everybody else will have more than they have now.

Now, let's face it - there are people who have accumulated vast amounts of money by *not* following these rules. That deserves a comment. One possible explanation is that what they do, what they provide, is either needed by or beneficial to mankind. These few individuals may unconsciously relate themselves to substance as it provides for the general improvement of the human race through evolutions of business and industry.

A hundred years ago, people such as Rockefeller, Carnegie, and J.P. Morgan were unconscious agents of the Supreme in developing industry. In more modern times, people such as Steve Jobs, the founder of Apple, and Bill Gates, the founder of Microsoft, come to mind.

I'm not saying that these folks did or did not follow the guidelines above. I'm only suggesting that in your quest to attract money, think of these folks as extremes; it's unwise to set your sights on playing in their leagues (at first). They're different for a reason, one which may not be easy to explain.

Their work is deemed a necessary part of our evolution. These individuals are like the dinosaurs of prehistoric times. They play a necessary part in the evolutionary process, but the power which produced them will ultimately dispose of them when their purposes are no longer useful.

It also doesn't hurt to dig into the private lives of some of these folks. They may have come into great wealth but many individuals in this class are absolutely miserable. They just haven't found the balance that we spoke of earlier. So don't be jealous of them. Do what you need to do to attract your own money.

It seems that money obtained on this plane of competition is often unsatisfactory, and it is not necessarily permanent. It's yours today and someone else may have it tomorrow. I've seen this again and again among business associates who play the "win-lose" game. They win now but later, they will lose.

Remember, if you are going to become rich in a scientific way, *The Money Miracle Way*, you must eliminate competition from your strategy. Don't think for a second that supply is limited. The minute you start thinking that all the money is being cornered and controlled by others, and that you have to fight this in order to get ahead, you will fall into a competitive mindset. Once you do that, your power to create disappears. What's worse, whatever creative movements you've already started may be stopped.

You should *know* that there are billions of dollars of untapped gold in the earth. Know that if all of these were found and mined, the universe would figure out a way to create or expose more in order to supply your needs. You should *know* that the money you need will come, even if a thousand people need to be led to discover new gold mines tomorrow to make it happen.

In other words, don't focus on the supply that is visible. Look at unlimited riches in the universe and *know* that they are going to come to you as fast as you can receive and use them. Nobody can keep you from getting what is yours by cornering the supply of visible wealth. Nobody!

So, never allow yourself to think for a second that all the best building lots will be taken before you are ready to build your house. Never worry about big corporations ending up owning the whole world. Never be afraid that you will lose what you want because somebody else "beat you to it." That just can't happen if you give up the competitive mindset. You are not looking for anything that someone else already owns. You are causing what you want to be created from the universe and the supply is limitless.

Stick to the statement that I previously gave you (which we'll build on in future chapters):

There is a thinking stuff from which all things are made and which, in its original state, permeates, penetrates, and fills every nook and cranny of the universe. A thought, held in this substance, produces the thing that is imaged by the thought. People can form things in their thoughts and, by impressing their thoughts upon formless substance (aka the universe), they can cause the things they think about to be created.

Chapter 6
How Money Flows to Me, and How It Will Flow to You

"The scientific use of thought consists in forming a clear and distinct mental image of what you want; in holding fast to the purpose to get what you want; and in realizing with grateful faith that you do get what you want."

(Wallace D. Wattles, American, Co-author of this book, 1860-1911)

Remember what I told you before, that for this stuff to work, you do not need to make sleazy "win-lose" deals. In fact, it absolutely won't work if that's how you play.

Now, I do not mean that you do not have to make deals at all. I do not mean that you don't have to have dealings with others. What I mean is that you won't need to deal with them unfairly. You don't have to try to get something for nothing. In fact, it's important to make sure that you give more to every person than you take.

Let's think this through. You can't buy something and give the seller more *money* than it's worth - at least not consistently. That's unsustainable. However, you can give s o m e o n e more in "use value" than the cash value of whatever you buy from her.

As an example, if you bought this book in paperback form; the paper, ink, and other material in it may not be worth what you paid. However, if the ideas in the book bring you thousands of dollars, euros, pounds, or any other currency, or many times that; then you got a pretty good deal! You will have received an excellent "use value" for a small amount of cash.

Let's suppose that I own an original signed painting by one of my favorite artists, Thomas Kinkade, worth thousands of dollars. I take it to a poor region in Africa and talk some locals into giving me $3,000 worth of handmade goods for it. I have really wronged the locals. They have no use for the painting. It has no value to them, and there is no market for them to liquidate it.

But if I give them $3,000 worth of water purification systems and water purification tablets for their handmade goods, then we've both made a good deal. The water purification systems will add to their lives in every way. In a sense, the systems will make them "rich."

When you leave the competitive plane and rise to the creative plane, you have an opportunity to re-evaluate your business operation. If you find yourself selling anything that doesn't add more to the buyer's life than what they give you in return, you can afford to stop (and you *must* stop). You do not have to beat anybody in business. If you are in a business that beats people, get out of it now!

Give every person more in use value than you take from him in cash value. Then, you are adding to the life of the world with every transaction you do.

If you have people working for you, it's necessary for you to take more from them in cash value than you pay them. However, you can set up your business in such a way that each person who works for you can improve his future earning potential through good experience. You can make your business do for your employees what this book is doing for you. You can make your business into a "ladder" of sorts, so that every employee who wants to can climb to riches herself. Given the opportunity to climb; if he won't do it, it's not on you!

And finally, just because you are to "cause" the creation of your riches from the universe, it does not mean that the things you want are going to simply appear out of the atmosphere right before your eyes. If you want a brand new Dodge Charger, for example, you don't just impress the thought of that fine vehicle on the universe until the car magically appears with a clear title in your driveway.

But if you do want that car, hold the mental image of it with absolute certainty that it is being made on the assembly line, and that it is on its way to you. Once you've formed the thought, you must have the most absolute and unquestioning faith that the car is coming. Don't think of it or speak of it in any other way other than that it is certain to come your way. Claim it as already yours. It will be made on the assembly line, if it hasn't been made already. It will be brought to you by the power of the universe, acting through the minds of people.

If you live in Maine, maybe a person from Texas or Japan will engage with you in some type of business deal that will result in your getting what you want. If it happens that way, the whole thing will be as much to the other person's advantage as to yours (remember the rules). Don't forget that the universe is in constant communication with everyone in it. It's not all just about you.

The desire of the universe for fuller life and better living has caused the creation of all the nice cars ever made, and it can cause the creation of many more. It will, whenever people set it in motion by desire and faith, and when they act in *The Money Miracle Way,* you can absolutely have that Dodge Charger in your driveway. You can also have anything else that you want, and that you will use it for the advancement or betterment of both your own life and the lives of others.

Don't hesitate to think and ask *big*. Jesus said, "It is your Father's pleasure to give you the kingdom." The universe wants you to have as large of a life as possible. It wants you to have all that you can use for living the most abundant life. If you sincerely believe that whatever you want is consistent with the desire of the universe for fuller and more complete expression, your faith becomes invincible.

Once I saw a little boy trying to play the piano. He was hitting the keys but not making anything that you could call music. He was a little angry because of this. I asked him why he was upset. He said, "I can feel the music in me, but I just can't make my hands go right." The music he felt in him was the *urge* of the universe, present with all the possibilities of life.

It was simply trying to seek expression through that child. God, the One Substance, is trying to live, and do, and enjoy things through humanity. He is saying, "I want people to build nice buildings, to play excellent music, to paint pictures. I want people's feet to run my errands; their eyes to see the beauty I've created, their tongues to tell all the great truths and sing beautiful songs," and so on.

Everything that is possible looks for its expression through people. The universe wants you to have a piano if you can play it, or any other instrument you can play. It wants you to have the means to cultivate your talents to the fullest extent. If you can appreciate beauty, it wants you to be able to surround yourself with beautiful things. If you can discern the truth, it wants you to have every opportunity to travel and observe. If you can appreciate good clothes, it wants you to own them. If you can appreciate good food, it wants you to eat it.

It wants all these things because it's how the universe can enjoy and appreciate them; it is the universe who wants to play and sing, and enjoy beauty and proclaim truth, and wear fine clothes and eat good food.

That desire that you feel for riches is the infinite, seeking to express Himself in you just as He tried to find expression through that little boy at the piano. So don't hesitate to think and ask big. Your role is to visualize and express the desire to God. This is very hard for many people. They hang on to that old idea that poverty and self-sacrifice are somehow pleasing to God.

They look on poverty as part of the plan, a necessity of nature. They have the idea that God has finished His work, and made all that He can make, and that the majority of people must stay poor because there is not enough to go around. They hang on to this erroneous thought so hard that they simply feel ashamed to ask for money or the things it buys. They try not to want more than just a meager existence, just enough to make them comfortable.

I hope you don't do this. As I've said before, the principles in this book are compatible with most spiritual belief sets. I hope you find that to be the case with yours.

I'm reminded of a student who I told that he must get in mind a clear picture of the things he desired, so that the creative thought of them might be impressed on the universe. He was reasonably broke, living in a rented house and having only what he earned from day to day. He just couldn't grasp the idea that all wealth, or even any wealth, was his for the asking.

So after thinking it over, he decided that what he really wanted was a new rug for the floor of one room of his rented house. He also wanted a space heater to take some of the bite off during the winter, because he could only afford to run his furnace on low.

He followed the instructions that I have laid out in this book and obtained both of these things in a few months. Then it dawned on him that he possibly should have asked for more. He went through the rented house and made a list of all the improvements he wanted to make. He mentally added new paint here and kitchen or bath upgrades there, until the pictures were clear in his mind as the ideal home. Then he planned his furnishings to make the home complete.

Holding these pictures in his mind, he began living in *The Money Miracle Way*, and moved toward what he wanted. Today, he owns the house. He is rebuilding it according to that mental image. Now, with even larger faith, he is going on to get even greater things. He's been given according to what he believed he would receive. It's the same for you, me, and everyone.

Chapter 7
Your Parents Were Right – Why Gratitude is Critical!

He is a wise man who does not grieve for the things which he has not, but rejoices for those which he has."

(Epictetus, Greek philosopher, circa 55-135)

Hopefully, I made it clear in the last chapter that the *first* step toward attracting money is to convey what you want, in a mental image format, to the universe. It is essential that you communicate with the universe in a peaceful, friendly, harmonious way. Such harmony is critical to your success.

I'm going to give you some steps to follow. If you follow them, they will bring you into perfect mental alignment with God. The whole process can be summed up in one word: *gratitude*!

Here are the steps:

1. You believe that there is one intelligent substance from which everything flows.
2. You believe that this substance gives you everything you truly want.
3. You relate to it by having and holding a feeling of deep and profound gratitude.

Many people who live their lives right and who follow *most* of *The Money Miracle Way*, end up staying broke due to their lack of gratitude. They've received one gift from God, and they cut the "supply chain" through which that gift traveled by failing to acknowledge it.

Let me give you an example, one which I am guilty of and you may be too. I once lived in a fairly small house, drove an old car, had a modest income and a lot of bills. I asked for more; I prayed for more; I made it my intention to have more. But in the process of doing these things, I failed to acknowledge that I already *had* a decent little house, a modest car, an okay income, enough food to put on a few extra pounds, and so on. I focused on what I wanted, without being the least bit grateful for what I already had (in fact, I was very *ungrateful* for it).

Don't misunderstand - you don't need to be satisfied with what you have, just be grateful for it as if it were a step along the way (because it is)!

In a manner of speaking, the closer we "live" to the source of wealth, the more wealth we are likely to receive. The soul that is always grateful is likely to "live" closer to God than the one which never bothers to be thankful to Him. The more gratefully we fix our minds on the Supreme when good things come to us, the more good things we will receive and the faster they will come! It's not rocket science - a mental attitude of gratitude brings your mind closer to the source from which the blessings come.

If this whole "attitude of gratitude" idea that gratitude brings your whole mind in closer harmony with the creative energies of the universe seems strange to you; give it serious thought and I'm sure you'll find that it is true. Whatever you have now that is good came to you in accordance with certain universal "laws," not just because you are awesome or deserving (even though both may also be true). Gratitude will take your mind down the path along which things travel to get to you. It will keep you in close harmony with creative thought and prevent you from falling into the trap of competitive thought.

Only gratitude can keep you looking above and prevent you from falling into another trap, a trap of thinking that supply is limited. If you were to fall into that trap, it would kill your hopes. This gratitude thing has a name - the Law of Gratitude. It's essential that you obey the law, if you want to get results. The Law of Gratitude is simply the natural principle that action and reaction are always equal, and in opposite directions.

So, the act of you mentally reaching out in thankful praise to the Supreme is actually an expenditure of force. It can't help but reach that to whom it was addressed; and the reaction of the

Supreme is an instantaneous movement back toward you.

There is a proverb, "Draw nigh unto God, and He will draw nigh unto you." That's some pretty outdated language but I think it means that a failure to be thankful yields a failure to get more. There is psychological truth to this statement. If your gratitude is both strong and constant, the reaction of the universe will also be strong and continuous. The movement of the things you want will always be toward you.

You cannot exercise very much power without gratitude. It is gratitude that keeps you connected to power! But understand - there is more value in gratitude than just using it as a tool to get more of what you want. Without gratitude, it won't take long before you are unsatisfied with the way things are.

The minute you start to dwell on the current situation being unsatisfactory, that's when you actually start to fall backward. You start fixating on the common, the ordinary, the poor; and your mind starts to take the shape of these things. Then, you will unknowingly transmit these images to the universe and the common, the ordinary, and the poor will come to you. If you allow your mind to dwell on the inferior, you will become inferior and will surround yourself with inferior things.

Ever wonder why some people seem to do everything right and yet just can't get ahead? Do you remember me (above) with my little house, my modest car, etc.? The thankful version of me looks back on those days with profound gratitude. It was a fun little house, the modest car shuttled my family to some great times, and the whole experience was a building block on the road to where I am today. But at the time, I felt I was stuck in a rut and just couldn't figure out why. Now we both know - I was trying to improve my life through angry expectation rather than joyful hope.

If you fixate on the best, you will begin to surround yourself with the best and to become the best. The creative power inside of us makes us into the image that we fixate on! In a sense, we are the universe, and the universe always takes the form that it thinks about.

The grateful mind constantly fixates on the best. Therefore, it tends to become the best. It takes the shape or the character of the best, and it will receive the best.

Also, faith is born of gratitude. The grateful mind continually expects good things. That expectation becomes faith. When you have gratitude in your own mind, that produces faith. Every outgoing "wave" of grateful thanksgiving increases faith.

If you have no feeling of gratitude, it would be difficult for you to maintain any kind of faith for long. Without faith, you can't attract money by the creative method, as you'll learn in the following chapters. So, it is necessary to form and cultivate the habit of being grateful for every good thing that comes to you - even something as simple as finding a penny on the street!

Give thanks continuously. If you're in the habit of praying, consider adding gratitude to your prayers. Since everything that has come to you has contributed to your growth and advancement, be sure to include everything in your expressions of gratitude.

By the way, don't waste time thinking or talking about the shortcomings or wrongdoings of government leaders or the über wealthy. A lot of your opportunity was created by them and the things they've done, even if you believe it was unintentional. Don't spend a lot of time bad-mouthing politicians, including the ones you may believe are corrupt. If it weren't for politicians, even bad ones, we would have anarchy and you would have even less opportunity.

God has worked hard and waited patiently for the world to come to its current state. He's going to continue right on with his work. At some point, he'll do away with those that don't use their wealth for good and those who don't properly use their political power. But in the meantime, hard as it may seem, envision them as being good. They are helping arrange the "transmission lines" along which your riches can come to you. Be grateful to them for being partners in your personal quest. This will help you come into harmony with the good in everything, and the good in everything will move toward you.

Chapter 8

How to Think – *The Money Miracle Way*

"The starting point of all achievement is DESIRE. Keep this constantly in mind. Weak desire brings weak results, just as a small fire makes a small amount of heat."

(Napoleon Hill, American author, 1883-1970)

Please look back to Chapter 6, and re-read the story of the man who formed the mental image of his house. It's OK - do it now. We'll wait. This will give you a good idea of the first step toward attracting money.

It's crucial that you form a clear and definite mental picture of what you want. (One way to do this is to create an actual image on paper of what it might look like, and refer to it intently and frequently.) You cannot transmit an idea until it is burned into your brain.

You must *have* the idea before you can *give* the idea. Many people are unable to impress their idea on the universe because they only have a foggy idea of what they want to do, to have, or become. Think about yourself - does this describe you? Or do you have a clear, visual, mental image of the future?

Don't even think about just having a desire to have a lot of money so that you can do good with it. News flash - not good enough! *Everyone* has that desire!

You can't just wish to travel, see things, do more, etc. Everyone wants those things too. If you were going to send a text to a friend, you would not send him the letters in the alphabet and hope that he would put the message together himself. Nor would you simply send him a bunch of random words from the dictionary.

You would (hopefully) put together a coherent thought or sentence, one which had some meaning. It's the same thing when you try to impress your desires on the universe. You must do it with a coherent statement. You must know what you want, and you must be definite about it.

The famous author Dr. Joe Vitale has described it as the universe as a catalog, and you get what you want by simply placing your order. But think of the last time you really placed an order from a catalog. You ordered the exact item, size, shape, color, and quantity that you wanted - you did not simply go to the seller's web site and order "a whole lot of stuff." It's the same principle here.

You can never get rich or even start the process, by sending out vague concepts of your wishes. Go over your wants just like the guy with the house did. See exactly what you want. Get a clear mental picture of it as you want it to look when you get it.

You need to keep your clear mental picture continually in mind. I'm a bit old fashioned; I actually have a three ring binder with a picture on each page of a thing I want, a place I want to travel to, what my mortgage looks like with the word "paid" stamped on it, etc. I refer to them regularly, which makes it easier to keep those images burned in my mind.

Whether you do this or choose some other approach, it's *not* necessary to do concentration exercises. It's not necessary to set aside special times for prayer (at least, not for this purpose). It's not necessary to meditate (at least, not for this purpose). *For this purpose, you simply need to know exactly what you want, and want it so badly that it stays in your thoughts.*

You should spend a fair amount of your leisure time thinking about your picture. However, you don't need to practice mind control exercises of any type to concentrate on something you really want. It takes effort to concentrate on the things you *don't* want, not on the things you want.

Unless you really want to attract money, enough so that you can keep the idea foremost in your thoughts, it won't be worth your trouble to even try what we've outlined in this book. These methods are only for people who want it so badly that they are willing to overcome mental laziness and work for it. (Yes, it's easy, but it does still require work.)

The more clear and definite your mental picture is (which is why I use real pictures) and the more you dwell on it and savor its delightful details, the stronger your desire will be. The stronger your desire, the easier it will be to keep your mind fixed upon the picture of what you want.

There is still a bit more to it than this, though. There's more to it than just seeing the picture clearly. If all you do is see the picture clearly, you're just a dreamer and you won't make it happen. In addition to your clear vision, you must have a *definiteness of purpose behind it*. Behind that purpose, you must have an unwavering faith, not that you *will* receive or accomplish it but that you *already have* achieved or accomplished it. It's yours. It's done. Good work. Enjoy it.

If your vision is a new house, live in it mentally until it takes a physical form around you. If your goal is a college diploma, walk down the aisle on graduation day mentally and claim that diploma - and believe that it's real! Enjoy the things you want before they come to you, and they will.

Remember the words of Jesus, "Whatsoever things you ask for when you pray, believe that you receive them, and you shall have them." (Note that Jesus said, "Believe that you *receive* them." He did not say, "Believe that you *will* - or *might*, or deserve to - receive them.")

I can't stress this strongly enough. See what you want as if it is already there, not as if it will be there. See yourself owning and using what you want. Use them in your imagination just as you will use them when you actually have them. Mentally drive that Mercedes to work before you own it. Mentally cook in that huge kitchen before your dream house is built. This is critical.

Dwell upon your mental picture until it is crystal clear. Then take a mental attitude that you already own everything in that picture. Take possession of it in your mind, with the full faith that it is already yours.

Hold on to this mental ownership. Don't waver for a second. It's yours; you've achieved it; now enjoy it. Your faith must be absolutely real.

These last few paragraphs may be the most important in the book, so I hope you consider them carefully. Some people have a problem acting as though they've already *received* something.

Here's the paradox. If you want something and you act as if you *will* receive it, then you are coming from a place of lack (of the thing that you want), and you're sending an image to the universe of *not* having the thing that you want. So there is a tendency to attract more of *not* having it. Act as if you have received it and already have it, and there will be a tendency to attract what you want. Try this with something small and watch it work.

And don't forget what I told you in the last chapter about gratitude. You should be as thankful for it during this time as you expect to be when it actually takes form. The person who can sincerely thank God for the things which he only owns in his imagination has genuine faith. He will attract money and the things it buys; he will cause the creation of whatever he wants.

You don't need to pray repeatedly for what you want. You don't need to tell God about it every single day. Jesus said, "Use not vain repetitions as the heathen do, for your Father knows that you have need of these things before you ask Him."

Your job is to intelligently formulate your desire for the things which will make your life larger and better, and to get those desires arranged into a coherent whole. (Again, this is why I use the three ring binder with pictures of all my key desires in it. Each page represents a piece; the binder itself represents the whole.)

Once you've arranged them into a whole, your job is to impress the whole upon the universe, which has the power and will to bring you what you want. You don't make this impression by repeating strings of words. You do it by holding a vision with unshakable *purpose* to achieve it and with unwavering *faith* that you do (not will, but do) attain it. The answer to your prayers is not according to your faith while you are talking, but according to your faith while you are working toward your goals.

You cannot impress the mind of God by having a special "holy day" to tell Him what you want, and then forgetting him the rest of the week. You cannot impress Him by having special hours to go into your closet and pray, if you then forget the subject until the next prayer time.

Don't misunderstand me. Oral prayer is good and valuable. It can help you clarify your vision and strengthen your faith. However, oral prayer is not the best path to getting the things you want. In order to attract money, you don't need a "sweet hour of prayer." You need to "pray without ceasing." And by "pray," I mean holding steady to your vision, with a vision of making it take form. You must simultaneously hold the faith that you *are* making it take form. "Believe that you receive them."

The key, then, is not in the wanting but in the receiving. Once you've clearly formed your vision, you must focus on having achieved it. It is good to make an oral statement, addressing the Supreme in reverent prayer. From that moment forward, though, you must receive what you have asked for. Don't hope for it, don't dream about it, don't think about how nice it would be. Receive it and enjoy it.

Live in the new house. Wear the new clothes. Drive the Bentley to work. Enjoy the trip to China and plan future trips with confidence.

Think and speak of things you ask for in terms of actually having them. Imagine your environment and your financial condition exactly as you want them.

At the same time, however, be careful not to become just a dreamer. Hold on to unwavering *faith* that what you are imagining is in the process of being realized. Remember that it is faith and purpose in the use of the imagination that makes the difference between the achiever and the dreamer.

And having learned this, the next step is to learn the proper use of your *will*, which we will do in the next chapter.

Chapter 9
Where There is a Will, There is a Way

"Will is character in action."

William McDougall, British - American psychologist,
1871 - 1938)

If you want to systematically attract money, you don't need to try to apply your willpower to anyone or anything outside yourself. In fact, you have no *right* to do that. It is wrong to apply your will to others, in order to get them to do what you want done. It is just as wrong to coerce people by mental power as it is to coerce them by physical power.

If compelling people by physical force to do what you want makes them slaves, compelling them by mental force does exactly the same thing. The only difference is in your method.

If taking things from people by physical force is robbery, taking things by mental force is also robbery. In principle, there is no difference.

You have no right to use your willpower on another person, even "for his own good." In spite of what you think, you don't actually know what is for his own good.

The science of attracting money does not require you to apply power or force to any other person, in any way whatsoever. There isn't even the slightest need to do so. In fact, any attempt to use your will on others will actually defeat the purpose.

You don't need to apply your will to things to get them to come to you. That would simply be trying to coerce God - which would be foolish, useless, and irreverent.

You don't need to compel God to give you good things, any more than you have to use your willpower to make the sun rise. You don't need to use your willpower to conquer an unfriendly deity or to get the devil to do your bidding.

The universe is friendly to you, and is even more anxious to give you what you want than you are to get it. To attract money, you need to use your willpower on yourself! When you know what to think and do, then you need to force yourself to think and do the right things. That's the proper way to use your will to get what you want - use it to keep yourself on the right course.

Use your will to keep yourself thinking in *The Money Miracle Way*. Don't try to project your will, your thoughts, or your mind out into space; to make it "act" on things or people. Keep your mind here at home. It can accomplish more here than anywhere else.

Use your mind to form a mental image of what you want. Hold that vision with faith and purpose. Use your will to keep your mind working in *The Money Miracle Way*.

The more steady and continuous your faith and purpose, the more rapidly you will attract money, because you will make only positive impressions on the universe. Also, you will not neutralize or offset any of the positive impressions with negative impressions.

The picture of your desires, if you hold it strong with faith and purpose, will be taken up by the universe. Where it actually goes, I haven't a clue. It could travel a billion miles for all I know.

I *do* know that as the impression spreads, things are set in motion to make the picture real. Every living thing, every inanimate thing, and even the things not yet created are urged towards "creating" what you want. Mysterious forces begin to be exerted in that direction. Everything begins to move towards you. The minds of people everywhere are influenced toward doing what is needed to fulfill your desires; and they work for you unconsciously.

Powerful stuff, isn't it?

Now, you can destroy the whole deal by impressing a *negative* thought on the universe. (I completely quit all forms of complaining a few years ago, and you're about to learn why.) Any amount of doubt or unbelief will start things moving *away* from you, just as surely as faith and purpose will start moving things *towards* you.

Remember the last day you had when *everything* went wrong? Think hard. I'll bet it didn't start with *everything* going wrong. I'll bet it started with one thing which you dwelled on a bit; then another negative thing happened. You reinforced your bad day by dwelling on that. Things went downhill from there. Does that about sum it up? I'll bet it does. It's something to think about.

Because people don't understand this, they feel the need to use "mental science" to attract money, which usually ends in failure. Every hour, minute, and second you spend wallowing in doubts and fears; every hour you spend in worry; every hour in which your soul is surrounded by unbelief; moves things in a current away from you rather than toward you.

Belief is all-important. For that reason, it is critical to guard your thoughts. Since your beliefs will be shaped to a large extent by the things you see and think about, it is important to manage what you think about. Here is where your will becomes a factor, because it is through your will that you determine what your mind will focus on.

If you want to attract money, don't study poverty. Things don't come to you by thinking about the opposite of what you want. You won't be the picture of health by studying and focusing on disease. You won't be righteous by studying and thinking about sin. It follows, then, that nobody has ever attracted money by studying and thinking about poverty.

Medicine, as a science of disease, has in many ways increased disease. Religion as a science of sin has in many ways increased sin. Likewise, studying economics by focusing on poverty will result in more poverty.

Don't talk about poverty. Don't investigate it. Don't concern yourself with it. Never mind what its causes are - you have nothing to do with them. What should concern you is the cure.

I have the privilege of providing some financial support to a young lady in a (largely) third world country - Guatemala. She is eighteen, the youngest of ten children, and going to college to make a life for herself and her parents. She has a clear set of goals and solid plans on how to get there. I have the opportunity, through a wonderful organization, to help her reach those goals by providing modest monthly financial support during her college years.

Notice I did not describe anything unpleasant about her living conditions or those in her neighborhood. They're all irrelevant. What counts is that she is going - not attempting, but going, to make a better life for herself and her parents, and it's my honor to help her get there.

Now, as you think about how strongly I've urged you not to focus on poverty, and you're wondering just what a cold-hearted guy I must be for saying that, let me clarify. I don't mean at all that you should be cold-hearted or unkind. I don't mean that you should refuse to hear the cries of need.

What I am saying is that you should not try to eradicate poverty in conventional ways. It won't work. Put poverty behind you. Put all that poverty represents behind you, and "make good." Attract money and do good with it. That's the best way you can help the poor. The challenge is, you can't hold the mental image of attracting money if you fill your mind with pictures of poverty. It won't work.

Don't read books that show pictures or tell the stories of slum dwellers, the horrors of sex slavery, and so on. Don't read anything at all which fills your mind with gloomy images of want and suffering. You can't help the poor by studying these things; and having a good knowledge of them won't help you do away with poverty.

Getting pictures of poverty into your mind does not help eradicate poverty. Get- ting pictures of wealth into the minds of the poor is the better approach (such as my young friend in Guatemala did long before I was introduced to her). Just because you refuse to allow your mind to be filled with pictures of the misery that is poverty, you are *not* deserting the poor.

Poverty can't be eliminated by increasing the number of people who think about poverty. It can only be eliminated by increasing the number of poor people who develop an absolute intention, backed by faith, to attract money and get out of poverty. (Those who continue to think poor, will continue to be poor.)

The poor need inspiration much more than they need charity. Charity sends them food for the moment or gives them money to support a habit that will help them forget for a couple of hours. Inspiration will help them to rise out of their misery. If you want to help the poor, teach them that they can rise out of their condition (again, remember my friend in Guatemala). After you teach them this, prove it to them by attracting money yourself.

The only real way to begin eradicating poverty is to start getting more and more people to practice the teachings of this book. People must be taught to attract money by creation, not by competition. Every time someone attracts money by competition, he throws down the very ladder he climbed, thus keeping others down.

On the other hand, everyone who attracts money by creation opens a way for many others to follow him/her, and inspires them to do so. You are not being hard-hearted or unfeeling when you refuse to pity poverty, see poverty, read about poverty, think about poverty, or listen to those who talk about poverty. Use your will power to keep your mind off the subject of poverty, and to keep it fixed with faith and purpose on the vision of what you want.

Chapter 10

Where There's a Will, There's a Way (Part II)

"'Tis in ourselves that we are thus or thus. Our bodies are our gardens to which our wills are gardeners."

(William Shakespeare, British playwright, 1564 - 1616)

As we've said, you want to retain a clear vision of money and the things it will buy. However, you can't do this if you constantly have opposing images in your brain, whether they are real or imaginary. If you've had past financial difficulties, don't talk about them and don't think of them. If your parents were poor and things were rough early in your life, don't talk about or think of them.

We humans are gifted with the ability to revise history and you must do just that. Otherwise, to think and speak of poverty will mentally classify you now as being in that situation. That will definitely slow your progress towards money. They say that our memories of the past are not nearly as accurate as we think - so why not change our memories of the past to make it very positive?

This is why you won't hear any "rags to riches" stories about me. I've always been blessed -

even when I had the little house I told you about in previous chapters. The blessings are just bigger now!

Put poverty and the things that pertain to poverty completely behind you. If you're following my guidance, then you've accepted a theory of the universe as being right.

You're resting all your hopes of future happiness and prosperity on it being right. So what can you possibly gain by allowing ideas that conflict with this theory into your head?

What I'm teaching you is compatible with most religions—but not all. You've got a decision to make. If you want to believe that the world is coming to an end soon, or that there are limited resources, or that it's inappropriate for you to want to attract money, you might as well put this book down because what we are teaching here won't work. Don't read anything pessimistic, including anything that implies that the whole world is going down the tubes.

There may be many things in the world which are disagreeable. It's always been that way throughout history. What's the use of studying the bad? If you're looking at things the right way, the bad is only passing by anyway but studying it tends to keep it with us. Why study things that are being phased out by positive evolution? The only way you can help get rid of them is to help that evolution move faster.

Conditions may seem terrible in certain countries, regions, or places. However, you are wasting your time and destroying your own chances by dwelling on those things. Make up your mind to help people in the world to attract money. Think of all the riches the world is coming into, instead of the poverty it is growing out of. Keep in mind that the only way you can help the world to attract money is to do so yourself through the creative method, not the competitive one.

Focus totally on riches. Ignore poverty. That doesn't mean you have to ignore poor people. But when you think or speak of them, think or speak of them as people who are attracting the money to improve their conditions; as those who should be congratulated rather than pitied. That can help them and others catch your inspiration, and search for the way out of their situation. Are you getting this? You don't have to be mean. You just need to change the way you project your thoughts on the subject.

Attracting lots of money is one of the most honorable and worthwhile goals you can have in life because it encompasses just about everything else. Remember, though, that the struggle to attract money on the competitive plane is nothing but a godless scramble for power over others. When you shift into the creative mind, everything changes.

Everything that is possible on this earth becomes possible by attracting money; it all becomes possible by the use of things. If your health is poor, for example, it will likely take a lot of money to improve it. It's very difficult to have great health if you are wallowing in financial worry.

Moral and spiritual greatness can only happen to those who rise above the competitive battle for existence. Only those who are attracting money on the plane of creative thought can rise above the degrading influences of competition.

If your vision is one of having a great home life, remember that love lives best where there is a certain level of class, a high level of thought, and freedom from corrupting influences. Where money is attracted through creative thought, without strife or rivalry, these things can be found and you can have your great home life.

There is no more noble or greater a goal than to attract money. You must fixate on a mental picture of money and make sure it crowds out any conflicting images. You must learn to see the underlying truth in all things. You must see beneath all the seemingly wrong conditions.

In truth, at least in our truth, poverty does

not exist. There is only wealth. Unfortunately, many people remain in poverty because they simply don't know there is wealth for them. Your mission, if you choose to accept it, is to show them the way to affluence through your own behavior.

Many other people are poor because, while they feel there is a way out, they are just too mentally lazy to put out the effort to move forward. For those people, the best you can do to help is to get them motivated by showing them the happiness that comes from properly attracting money and the things it buys.

Others are poor because while they have some understanding of science, they've become swamped by often conflicting theories on how to attract money. They simply don't know which direction to go. They try a mixture of many systems, and fail in all of them. (If you've read more than two or three books on this subject that each teach a different approach, you know what I mean.) For these folks, again, the best thing you can do is show them the right way to go through your own behavior.

An ounce of actually doing things is worth a pound of theory. The very best thing you can do for the whole world is to make the most of yourself. You can serve your God and your fellow man in the best possible way by attracting money - through the creative method and not the competitive one.

Remember - the basis of this book is that it provides you, in detail, the principles of *the* science of attracting money. If you believe it, then you don't need to read any other book on the subject. This may sound egotistical and I'm sorry for that. But consider this: If you have a book that lays out the basic principles of beginning algebra, you don't need any other books on that subject.

There is only one scientific way to think and that is to think in the way that leads you most directly and simply to your goal. Nobody has formulated a briefer or less complex "system" than the one I've laid out in this book. It's been stripped of all the BS, all the non-essentials. When you decide to move forward with this process, put every other process out of your mind altogether.

Again, at the risk of sounding a little arrogant, I recommend that you read this book every day. Keep it with you. Commit it to memory. Don't think about other "systems" and theories. If you do, you'll begin to have doubts. Your thinking will begin to waver and you'll begin to have failures.

After you've done well and attracted lots of money through creativity, then you can study all the systems you want (though why would you want to?). But until you have everything you need, and know how to get anything you might need in the future, please don't read anything else on this topic that may be conflicting.

When you read the news, skim over the bad stuff and focus on the positive - the things that are in harmony with your own vision.

If you have interest in the occult, please defer it. Don't dabble in studies of spirits and such. It's not out of the question that the dead are still around us in some way - but if they are, leave them alone. Mind your own business.

Wherever the spirits of the dead may be, they've got their own issues. They've got their own work to do. We have no right to interfere with them. We can't help them and it's very unlikely that they can help us, or whether we even have a right to ask them to do so if they can!

Leave the dead and the hereafter alone, and meet your own challenge - attract money. If you begin to dabble in the occult, it will create mental cross-currents which will derail your dreams.

So, as we close out this chapter, I'd like to repeat our "thesis statement," slightly expanded from the last time you read it:

There is a thinking stuff from which all things are made and which, in its original state, permeates, penetrates, and fills every nook and cranny of the universe. A thought, held in this substance, produces the thing that is imaged by the thought. People can form things in their thoughts and, by impressing their thoughts upon formless substance (aka the universe), they can cause the things they think about to be created.

In order to do this, people must pass from the competitive to the creative mind; they must form a clear mental picture of the things they want and hold this picture in their thoughts with the fixed purpose to get what they want, and the unwavering faith that they do get what they want; closing their minds against whatever may tend to shake their purpose, dim their vision, or kill their faith.

Chapter 11

Living Life *The Money Miracle Way*

*"A man is but the product of his thoughts.
What he thinks, he becomes."*

(Mahatma Ghandi, Indian political leader, 1869-1948)

As we've said before, in effect, thoughts create things. Thinking in *The Money Miracle Way* will definitely help bring money your way.

That said, you can't rely on thought alone. There are certain physical actions that are required. This is where a lot of good, solid metaphysical thinkers crash and burn - they fail to connect thought and personal action!

We have not yet reached a stage of evolution, assuming such a stage is even possible, in which a person can create directly from the universe without the involvement of nature or human hands. People must not only think but must use personal actions to supplement their thought.

With thought, you can cause gold buried deep into the mountainside to begin moving toward you. However, it will not mine itself, refine itself, coin itself into Krugerrands, and come rolling down the road looking to find your pocket. Under the power of the universe, the affairs of the world will shift in such a way that someone will be led to the gold mine to mine the gold for you. The activities of others will shift so as to move the mined and minted gold in your direction. You in turn, must shift your own business affairs so that you can properly *receive* it when it comes to you.

Your thoughts can make things, both animate and inanimate, work to bring you what you want. However, your personal activities must be properly aligned with your thoughts so that you can properly receive it when it makes its way to you.

You must not take it as charity. You must not steal it. You must give every person more in "use value" than they give you in cash value. The scientific use of thought is in forming a clear and distinct mental image of what you want; in fixating on the desire and intention to get what you want; and in realizing with grateful faith that you do get what you want.

Don't try to "project" your thought in some mysterious way, with the idea that it will go out and do things for you. That's a waste of effort, and it will weaken your ability to think rationally. The importance of thought in the process of attracting money is fully explained in the previous chapters. Your faith and purpose positively impresses your vision upon the universe, which has the same desire for more life that you have. This vision, upon being received from you, sets all the creative forces in action, directed toward you.

It's not up to you to guide or supervise the creative process. All you have to do is to keep your vision, stick to your purpose, and keep your faith and gratitude. But you must act in *The Money Miracle Way*, so that you can grab what is yours when it comes to you. You need to be there when the things in your vision come to you, so that you can receive and process them appropriately as they arrive.

It's really not hard to see the truth in this. When something comes your way, before it is yours, it will be in the hands of someone else who will want to get paid for it. You can only get what is "yours" by giving the other person what is "his." Your wallet or purse is not going to be transformed into a limitless ATM, which is always spitting out money without any effort on your part.

This is the crucial point of the science of attracting money - right here, where thought and personal action must be combined. There are a lot of people who, consciously or unconsciously, set the forces in motion through the strength and persistence of their desires, but get nowhere because they are not properly prepared to *receive* what they have asked for!

Through the power of thought, the thing you want is brought to you. Through the power of action, you receive it. Whatever the action needs to be, you must do it *now*. You cannot act in the past, plus it's essential that you get the past out of your mind to keep your vision clear. You can't act in the future, because the future isn't here yet. You can't even know how you would act in the future under a certain set of circumstances, until and unless those circumstances arrive.

Just because you are not in the right business or the right environment at the present time, don't think it's okay to postpone action until you get into the right business or environment. It's not. And don't spend time in the present strategizing how to handle future contingencies. Have faith in your ability to handle those contingencies when/if they arrive.

If you act in the present with your mind in the future, then your action will be with a divided mind and it just won't be effective. Put your whole mind into action now. Don't give your creative impulse to the universe and then sit back and wait for results. If you do, they will never come.

Act now. There is never any time but now, and there never will be any time but now. If you are ever to begin to get ready to receive the things you want, you must begin now!

Your action, whatever it is, will most likely have to begin in your present business or environment, and it must involve the people and things surrounding your present environment. You can't act in a place where you aren't present. You can't act in a place where you may be in the future. You can only act where you are.

Don't worry about whether yesterday's work was done well or poorly. Do today's work well. Don't try to do tomorrow's work now. There will be plenty of time to do it tomorrow.

Don't try to impose your will on people or things that are out of your reach. Don't wait for a change of environment before you act. The point is, you can act now in order to change your environment.

Fix in your mind with faith and purpose the vision of you in that better place. At the same time, act on your present environment with all your heart, with all your strength, with all your mind. Don't spend your time daydreaming or building castles. Hold one vision of what you want and act *now*.

Don't start looking for some unusual approach, some strange action to perform as a first step to attracting money. For the near future, your actions will probably be the same as they've always been. However, you must begin to perform those actions now in *The Money Miracle Way*, which will surely cause you to attract money.

If you are involved in a business and it's not the right one for you, don't wait until you get into the right business before you begin to act. Don't feel discouraged. Don't sit down and pout because you feel you are lost. Nobody was ever so lost that he couldn't, sooner or later, find the right place. Nobody ever became so involved in the wrong business or profession that he couldn't get into the right business or profession.

Hold the vision of yourself in the right business, with the purpose of getting into it and keep the faith that you will get into it, and that you are getting into it. At the same time, act in your present business.

Use your present business as a means of getting a better one. Use your present environment as a means of getting into a better one. Your vision of the right business, if you hold it with faith and purpose, will cause the universe to move the right business toward you. Your action, if performed in *The Money Miracle Way*, will cause you to move toward the business.

If you have a job rather than a business and you feel that you must have a better job to get what you want, don't "project" your thought into space and rely on that to get you another job. It probably won't work. Instead, hold the vision of yourself in the job you want, while you act with faith and purpose on the job you have, and you're almost certain to get the job you want.

Your vision and faith will set the creative force in motion to bring it toward you, and your action will cause the forces in your own environment to move you toward it.

In closing this chapter, I'd like to add one new sentence to our thesis statement:

There is a thinking stuff from which all things are made and which, in its original state, permeates, penetrates, and fills every nook and cranny of the universe. A thought, held in this substance, produces the thing that is imaged by the thought. People can form things in their thoughts and, by impressing their thoughts upon formless substance (aka the universe), they can cause the things they think about to be created.

In order to do this, people must pass from the competitive to the creative mind; they must form a clear mental picture of the things they want and hold this picture in their thoughts with the fixed purpose to get what they want, and the unwavering faith that they do get what they want; closing their minds against whatever may tend to shake their purpose, dim their vision, or kill their faith.

In order for a person to receive what he/she wants when it comes, he/she must act now on the people and things in his/her present environment.

Chapter 12

Do it Now, If You Can Do it Right!

*"Start where you are. Use what you have.
Do what you can."*

(Arthur Ashe, American professional tennis player,
1943-1993)

In the previous chapters, we talked about how to use your thoughts. We talked about the fact that you need to begin now to do whatever you can where you are. You need to do *everything* that you can now, where you are.

You can move forward only by growing larger than you are now (metaphorically, of course). If you try to move forward without finishing your current jobs, you can't grow. The world grows by people filling and then outgrowing their current "places."

If nobody anywhere filled their present place, the world would go backwards. Those who don't quite fill their present place are dead weight to society, government, business, and industry. Others must carry them at great expense (this is a philosophical statement, not a political one.)

The progress of the world is slowed only by those who don't fill their current places. They belong to the old school, to a lower plane or stage of life. They tend to waste away.

No society could advance if every person was smaller than his place. Social evolution is guided by the laws of physical and mental evolution. In the animal world, evolution results from an excess of life. When some organism has more "life" in it than its own form can express, it moves to a higher plane through evolution and a new species is created.

There never would have been new species had it not been for organisms that more than filled their places. The law works the same for you. Your attracting money depends on your applying this principle. Every day is either a successful day for you, or one of failure. It is, of course, the successful days that get you what you want. If every day is a failure, you can never attract money. If every day is a success, you can't fail to attract all that you need and then some.

If something can be done today and you don't do it, then you've failed, at least in that respect. The consequences can be disastrous. You can't foresee the results of such a small act. You don't know the workings of all the forces that have been moving on your behalf. There may be a lot riding on you doing one simple thing. That may be the thing that opens the door to exceptional possibilities.

You can never know all the potential deals which the universe is making for you. If you fail to do some small thing, it may cause a long delay in getting what you want.

Every day, be sure to do everything that can be done that day. At the same time, remember this important limitation. You must not overwork and you must not rush blindly into doing the greatest number of things in the shortest possible time. It may be a little confusing but it's important to think it through.

You should not do tomorrow's work today. You should not try to do a week's worth of work in a day. It's really not the number of things you do, but the efficiency with which you do them that counts. Every act is, in itself, either a success or a failure. Every act is, in itself, either efficient or inefficient.

Every inefficient act is a failure. If you spend your life doing inefficient acts, your whole life will be a failure. The more things you do, the worse it will be, if every act is inefficient.

On the other hand, every efficient act is a success in itself. If every act of your life is an efficient one, your whole life must be a success.

The biggest cause of failure, then, is doing too many things inefficiently and not doing enough things efficiently.

If you do nothing that is inefficient and enough things that *are* efficient, you will attract lots of money. If you can figure out how to make every act an efficient one, then you will understand that attracting money is an exact science, like mathematics.

Can you make each separate act a success in itself? You can. You can make each act a success because the universe is working with you. The universe cannot fail. It is at your service. To make every act efficient, you only have to put power into it. Every act is either strong or weak. When every act is strong, you are acting in T*he Money Miracle Way* which will inevitably attract money to you.

So how do you make every act strong and efficient? Hold your vision while you act. Put the whole power of your faith and purpose into your vision. This is where most people fail, when they separate mental power from physical action. They use the power of the mind for a while and later, they take action. The two are not coordinated. So their acts are not successful in themselves. Too many of them are inefficient.

But if you put enough power into every act,

no matter how simple, every act will be a success in itself. Every success opens the door to more successes, as you move toward what you want. Your progress will become increasingly rapid.

Remember that successful actions have cumulative results. Since the desire for more life is everywhere, not just in us humans; when a person moves towards larger life, he gets help from his environment and his desire's influence is multiplied!

So, each day, do everything that you can do and do it efficiently. And when I say that you must hold your vision while you do each act, I don't mean that in an exact literal way. You don't need to focus on the vision in its smallest detail while you are doing the act. However, that the vision should always be at least in the back of your mind. In your spare time, you can focus on it more deeply until the details are firmly fixed into your memory. The more you do this, the quicker your results.

If you contemplate regularly, you will get a picture of what you want burned into your mind and firmly transferred to the mind of formless substance. That way, while you are actually working towards your goal, you will only need to mentally flash the picture in your mind to stimulate your faith and purpose, and cause you to give your best effort.

In your spare time, think about the picture in detail until your mind is so full of it that you can instantly flash on it. You will become so enthusiastic about the promises the image holds, that just quickly flashing on it will bring forth your highest energy level.

Let me repeat again our thesis statement, changing the ending just a little to help bring us to this point of the book.

There is a thinking stuff from which all things are made and which, in its original state, permeates, penetrates, and fills every nook and cranny of the universe. A thought, held in this substance, produces the thing that is imaged by the thought. People can form things in their thoughts and, by impressing their thoughts upon formless substance (aka the universe), they can cause the things they think about to be created.

In order to do this, people must pass from the competitive to the creative mind; they must form a clear mental picture of the things they want and hold this picture in their thoughts with the fixed purpose to get what they want; **and do, with faith and purpose, all that can be done each day, doing each separate thing efficiently.**

Chapter 13

How to Do What You Love

"Everyone has been made for some particular work, and the desire for that work has been put in every heart."

(Rumi, Persian poet and theologian, 1207-1273)

Your ability to succeed in any business or career will depend to some extent on your having the right skills for that business. You can't be a great music teacher without having, or at least understanding, good music skills. You can't be a good carpenter, plumber, or electrician without acquiring the skills of the trade. You can't be a good doctor without good medical skills.

But having good skills in your vocation does not guarantee that you will attract money. There are plenty of musicians with exceptional talent who are broke. There are plenty of highly skilled tradespersons who are broke. There are plenty of well-trained doctors and lawyers who are broke. There are plenty of business people who understand commerce and dealing with people who are broke.

Skills are tools. It's essential to have the tools, but it's also critical that they be used the right way. If a person wanted to build a custom piece of furniture, she could take a sharp saw, a square, a plane, etc. and build a really nice piece. Another person could take the same plans and the same tools, try to duplicate the effort and end up with a piece of junk. The second person probably doesn't know the right way to use the tools.

The skills of our mind are tools which you need to use to help you attract money. Of course, this process will be a lot easier if you get into a business or profession for which you have the right "mental tools."

In general, you will do best in the business or profession for which you have the best skills. You may think of this as the one that is the best "fit" for you. But this statement has limitations. Nobody should regard his/her job or business as being cast in stone, unable to be changed. You can attract money in any business because if you don't have the right talent, you can develop it. You just need to "make" your tools as you go along, rather than being stuck with just those that you were born with.

Of course, it's much easier for you to succeed in a job or business for which you already have good skills. But you can succeed in just about any job or business, because you can develop at least a basic talent to get your start down that road. There is nothing for which you can't develop at least a basic talent.

Again, you'll attract money most *easily* if you do the job or run the business for which you are the best fit. But you will attract money most *satisfactorily* if you do what you *want* to do.

Doing what you want to do is living. There is no real satisfaction in living if we are compelled to forever do what we *don't* want and can never do what we *do* want. You really could do *what you do* want to do. The fact that you want to do it is proof that you have the power to do it. Desire is nothing more than the manifestation of power.

A desire to be a musician, for example, is the power to be a musician, seeking its expression and development. A desire to be an inventor is mechanical talent seeking expression and development. Where is no power, either developed or undeveloped, there is no desire. On the other hand, where strong desire exists, that is proof that the power is strong and just needs to be developed properly.

Everything else being equal, it's best to choose the job or business for which you have the best skill. But if you have a strong desire to be in any particular profession, you should choose that as your ultimate goal. You can do what you want to do, and it's your right and privilege to be in the business or profession that you find most pleasant.

You are not obligated at all to do what you don't like to do. You should not do what you don't want, *except* as a way to get to what you do want. If mistakes caused you to be in a business or profession you don't like, you may need to do what you don't like to do for some amount of time. However, you can make your time there more pleasant by knowing that where you are is helping you to get where you are going.

If you feel that you are not in the right business or profession, don't act too quickly to try to get into another one. Generally, the best way to make the change is to grow into the new role. Don't be afraid to make a sudden or radical change if the opportunity presents itself, and you're certain it's the right opportunity. But never take sudden or radical action when you are in doubt as to the wisdom of that action.

There is never a hurry on the creative plane. There is no lack of opportunity. When you get out of the competitive mindset, you will understand that you never need to move too quickly. Nobody else is going to beat you to whatever you want to do. There is enough for everybody.

As a metaphor, if one parking space is taken, another one that's even better will open up for you shortly. There is plenty of time. When you are in doubt, wait. Reconsider your vision, and increase your faith and purpose. And don't forget, especially in times of doubt and indecision, to cultivate lots of gratitude.

Spend a day or two contemplating the vision of what you want, while being in deep thanksgiving for the fact that you are *already receiving it*. This will bring you into such a close relationship with the Supreme that you will make no mistake when you act.

There is a mind which knows everything. You can come into close harmony with that mind by faith and the purpose to move forward in your life. You just need to have deep and profound gratitude.

Mistakes come from acting too quickly. They also come from acting in fear and doubt, or in a way that is not focused on the right motive, which is more life to all and less to none. As you move forward in *The Money Miracle Way*, opportunities will simply begin to show up with increased frequency. You'll need to be very steady in your faith and purpose, and to keep in close contact with the universe with reverent gratitude.

Do everything you can, perfectly, every day. But do it deliberately, not too quickly, and do it without worry or fear. Go as fast as you can but never hurry! Remember that the minute you begin to hurry, you are no longer creating but rather competing. You drop back down to that old "competition" plane again.

Whenever you find yourself rushing, call for a time-out. Fixate on the mental image of the things you want and begin to give thanks that you *are receiving them*. The exercise of gratitude will never fail to strengthen your faith and renew your purpose.

Chapter 14
How the Whole World Can Grow

"As I grow older, I pay less attention to what men say. I just watch what they do."

(Andrew Carnegie, Scottish - American industrialist and money miracle creator, 1835-1919)

Whether or not you decide to change professions or businesses, you must still be in the present in your current profession or business. You can work your way into a change constructively through your current vocation, by doing your daily work in *The Money Miracle Way*. And to the extent that your current profession involves dealing with other people, whether in person or by phone/email, you must remember to convey to them the impression of increase.

"Increase" is what everyone wants. It is the urge of the universe within them, looking for fuller expression. The desire for "more" is pervasive in nature. It is the fundamental impulse of the universe.

Every activity in human life is based on the desire for increase. You may want more/better food, more clothes, a bigger house, more luxury, more knowledge, more beauty, or more pleasure. Increase is simply more life.

Every living thing has a tendency towards continuous advancement. When there is no more increase of life, there is death. Most people know this instinctively, which is why people are forever looking for more. The law of perpetual increase has biblical roots: Only those who gain more retain any; from him who has not shall be taken away that which he has; etc. The *normal* desire for more wealth is neither evil nor reprehensible. It is normal. It is simply the desire for more abundant life. It is aspiration, which is inherent in human nature.

Because wanting more is so deeply rooted in human nature, people are attracted to the source of abundance. By following *The Money Miracle Way* which we've described in this book, you will get continuous increase for yourself *and* you will give it to everybody you deal with at the same time!

You become something of the center of your universe and increase flows from you to everyone else. Be sure this happens. Be sure to let others know that this is your intention. No matter how small a transaction you are involved in, project thoughts of increase into the transaction and make sure the customer receives those vibes.

It's important to convey the impression of advancement with everything you do. You want everyone you touch to receive the impression that you are an "advancing man" (or woman), and that you advance everyone who deals with you. Even in social settings, when you have no thought of actually conducting business, you should give the thought of increase.

You can do this by simply holding an unshakable faith that you yourself are directly in the path of increase. Let this faith inspire, fill, and permeate every action you take. Do everything with the firm belief that you are an advancing person and that you are giving advancement to everybody.

Feel that you are attracting money. More importantly, feel that in the process, you are also making others attract money and giving benefits to everyone. Do not brag about your success. Don't talk about it unnecessarily. True faith is never boastful.

Whenever you find someone who brags, you should know that the person is secretly doubtful and afraid. Simply feel the faith and let it come through in every transaction. Let every act and every communication express a quiet assurance that you are attracting money in the quantities you desire.

Words will not be necessary to share that feeling with others. They will simply know it when they are in your presence and they'll continue to be attracted to you. Be sure to impress everyone you touch with the feeling that, by associating with you, they will get increase for themselves.

Remember to give them a "use value" that is greater than the cash value you are taking from them. Take a genuine pride in doing this and let everyone know it. If you do, you will have no lack of customers.

People will go where they know they will gain increase. The Supreme, which desires increase in all and which knows all, will move people toward you who have never heard of you. Your business will grow quickly and you'll be surprised at the unexpected benefits you'll receive. You'll be able to make bigger and bigger deals, gain a greater income and move into an even better business or profession if you want to. But remember to never lose sight of the vision of what you want, and your faith and purpose to get what you want.

This is a good time for a bit of caution regarding your motives. Be very careful to avoid the temptation to gain power over others. To the uninformed or the partially developed mind, nothing seems more pleasant. The desire to rule over others for our own purposes has been the curse of the world. Since the beginning of time, rulers have soaked the earth with blood in their battles to increase their turf. This does not seek more life for all; it only seeks more power for those rulers.

Today, the main motive in business and industry is the same. Corporations scramble for profits, often leaving the lives and hearts of people in their wake. Commercial kings, like political kings, are often overtaken by a lust for power.

Watch out for this temptation to have power, to become a "master," to be considered better than others, to impress others with opulence, etc. Hopefully, you can guess why by now - the mind that craves mastery over others is the competitive mind; and the competitive mind is not the creative one!

In order to master your own environment and your own destiny, it's not at all necessary for you to rule over others. In fact, if you do fall into this struggle for high places, you can begin to be conquered by fate and environment, and your ability to get rich becomes a matter of chance and speculation.

Beware of the competitive mind! Samuel M. Jones, an American politician in the 1800's and a staunch practitioner of "the golden rule," said it best, "What I want for myself, I want for everybody."

Chapter 15
How You Can "Grow" and Not Just "Get"

"Do the best you can in every task, no matter how unimportant it may seem at the time. No one learns more about a problem than the person at the bottom."

(Sandra Day O'Connor, American Supreme Court Justice, 1930 -)

The things we discussed in the last chapter apply to the professional, the businessperson, and the business owner alike. It doesn't matter if you are a physician, lawyer, teacher, or clergy person. If you can give increased life to others and make sure they are aware of it, they will be attracted to you and you will attract money.

The physician who holds the vision of herself as a great healer and who works toward the realization of that vision with faith and purpose, will become phenomenally successful. She'll have more patients than she can handle.

In fact, the field of medicine is a great example of people who can benefit from this process. People in medicine have the principle of healing in common, no matter what position or specialty they are in. The advancing person in medicine, who has a clear mental image of himself as successful and who obeys the laws of faith, purpose, and gratitude, is likely to be very successful in helping patients with the things that ail them.

The field of religion is another example. The world of the faithful is begging for clergy who can teach the science of abundant life. Those who master the science of attracting money, along with the related sciences of being well, being great, and having love; and who teach those sciences in conjunction with their spiritual messages will always have a congregation.

The world needs traditional spiritual teachings but it also needs these teachings. They will provide increase of life and people will gladly listen to them. Not only will they listen but they will strongly support the person who teaches them.

In addition to traditional spiritual teachings, we could use a demonstration of the science of life from the pulpit. The world could use preachers who not only *tell* us how to live but *show* us how to live. A preacher who is faithful as well as healthy, great, beloved, *and* is able to attract money in a good and proper way can show us how to develop those qualities in ourselves. When he shows up, he will have a large and loyal following.

The same can be said of an educator who can inspire students with the faith and purpose of advancing life. She will never be out of a job. Any teacher who has this faith and purpose can share it with her students. In fact, she can't help sharing it with them if it is part of her own life and practice.

The same is true of a lawyer, a business person, an artist, a dentist - of just about everybody!

These combined mental and personal actions that I've described are guaranteed to work. They can't fail. Every person who follows these instructions steadily, with perseverance, will attract money.

The law of *Increase of Life* is just as mathematically certain as the law of gravity. Attracting money is an exact science! If you are a salaried individual, you will find this just as true as anyone else. Don't feel that there is no chance of attracting money just because there is no visible opportunity for advancement or because you are working at a place where wages are small and the cost of living is high.

Remember to form your clear mental vision of what you want, and begin to act with faith and purpose. Do everything you can do toward your vision every day, and do each part of it in a perfectly successful way. Put the power of success and your purpose of attracting money and the things it buys into everything you do. But don't do this just with the idea of brown-nosing your employer or her bosses, in the hope that they will see your good work and move you ahead. That's not very likely.

The person who is simply a "good" worker, doing a "good" job and being satisfied with that is, in fact, valuable to his employer. It's not in the employer's interest to promote that person - he's probably worth more to the company exactly where he is!

To gain advancement, something more is necessary than to be too large for your place. The person who is sure to advance is the person who is too big for her place. She must have a clear concept of who she wants to be. She must know that she can become what she wants to be. Most importantly, she must be absolutely determined to be what she wants to be.

Don't try to grow larger than your present place just to please your employer. Do it for the purpose of advancing yourself. Hold the faith and purpose during work hours, after work hours, and before work hours. Hold it such that every person who comes in contact with you: manager, colleague, or social contact; will feel the power of purpose radiating from you. Do it so that everyone will "feel" advancement and increase when they are near you.

People will be attracted to you. If there is no possibility for advancement in your current job, an opportunity will appear for you to take a new job. There is a power which never fails to present an opportunity for the advancing person who is moving in obedience to law. God can't help helping you, if you act in *The Money Miracle Way*. He must do so, in a sense, to help Himself.

Nothing can keep you down. If you can't attract money in business, do it in agriculture or another field. If you begin moving in *The Money Miracle Way*, you can definitely escape your current world in business and end up where you want to be.

If enough people would start acting in *The Money Miracle Way*, businesses would have a huge problem. They would have to react by giving their workers more opportunity, or they would end up in financial trouble.

Nobody has to work for a thankless conglomerate. The conglomerates can keep the "worker bees" in hopeless conditions only as long as there are "worker bees" who are too stupid to know the science of attracting money or too lazy to practice it.

Start this method of thinking and acting, and your faith and purpose will soon show you an opportunity to better yourself. This opportunity will show up soon enough, because the Supreme will bring it to you.

However, don't wait for an opportunity to be everything you want to be. When an opportunity appears that will make you greater than you are now, and you are moved toward it, do it! That will be the first step toward even greater opportunity.

In this universe, lack of opportunity is impossible for a person living an advancing life. It's inherent in the "constitution of the cosmos" that everything will work for that person's benefit. It's a matter of "law" that he will attract money if he acts in *The Money Miracle Way*.

So, whether you are a wage-earner or a business owner, study this book carefully. Follow the actions I've laid out with confidence. I promise you, it will not fail.

Chapter 16
Watch Out For These Things!

"It is a good thing to learn caution from the misfortunes of others."

(Publilius Syrus, Syrian writer, circa 100 B.C.)

Some people will dismiss the idea that there is actually an exact science to attracting money.

Guess what? If they choose to believe that, they're right!

Some people believe that the supply of wealth is limited and that business and government must be radically changed before a large number of people can start doing well.

News flash - they're right too, if that's what they want to believe.

But these things are not true for the rest of us. True, some governments do their best to keep their people in poverty. However, consider this: None of the people who think in terms of limits are thinking and acting in *The Money Miracle Way.* If

126

they did, they'd separate themselves from the masses.

If everyone started moving forward as I've outlined in this book, neither governments nor business could stop them. In essence, the world order would have to change to accommodate the movement. If the people have an advancing mind, if they have the faith that they can attract money and the things they want, and move forward with the absolute purpose of achieving these goals, nothing can keep them in poverty.

People can shift gears into *The Money Miracle Way* at any time, under any government, and begin to attract money. When a large enough number of people do it under any government, they will automatically modify the system to pave the way for others. The more people who attract money on the *competitive* plane, the worse for others. However, the more who attract money on the *creative* plane, the better for others!

The best way to help the masses toward economic salvation is by getting a large number of people to practice the scientific method I've outlined in this book and attract money. This will show others the way. It will inspire them with a desire for a real life. It will give them the faith that it can be attained. It will give them the purpose to attain it.

For now, however, it is enough to know that neither your government nor the competitive system of business can keep you from attracting money. When you finally enter the creative plane of thought, you will rise above these things and become a citizen of another kingdom.

Just remember that you must think and act in the creative plane. Don't ever, even for a second, fall back into believing that the supply is limited. Don't ever, even for a second, slip back into the ways of competition.

When your thinking starts to drift in these directions, quickly correct it. When you are in a competitive mind, you've lost the cooperation of the universe.

Don't spend a lot of time planning to meet possible emergencies in the future. You should be concerned with doing today's work in a perfectly successful manner, and not with tomorrow's possible emergencies. You can deal with them when and if they show up.

Don't spend a lot of time worrying about how you will overcome obstacles which may be out on the horizon, unless it's crystal clear that you have to change course today to overcome them. No matter how big an obstacle may seem at a distance, you will find that if you operate *The Money Miracle*

Way, the obstacle will disappear as you approach it. Or, if it doesn't disappear, you will find a way over, through, or around it.

There is nothing that can defeat you if you are moving towards attracting money by following strictly scientific principles. If you obey the "law," you can't help but attract money, just as surely as you can't multiply two by two and get anything other than four.

Don't worry about possible disasters, obstacles, panics, or unfavorable circumstances. You'll have enough time to deal with those when they show up. You'll also find, when they do arrive, that they will bring along with them the potential for solution.

Watch your mouth. Don't ever speak of yourself, your business, or of anything else in a negative, discouraged, or discouraging way. Never, ever admit the possibility of failure. Don't speak in a way that implies failure as an option.

Don't speak of times being hard or of business conditions as being doubtful, even during a recession. Times may be hard and business doubtful for people on the competitive plane. For you, that's impossible. You can create what you want and you are above fear.

When others are having hard times and poor business, that's where you can find your greatest opportunities. Train yourself to think of and look at the world as something which is advancing and growing. Always speak in terms of advancement. If you do anything else, you are denying your faith in advancement. If you deny your faith in advancement, I promise you will lose it.

Don't ever allow yourself the luxury of feeling disappointed. You won't always get what you want when you want it and this may appear like failure to you. But if you hold to your faith, you will find that failure is a temporary illusion. Move forward in *The Money Miracle Way* and if you don't get what you want, know that you will get something so much better that it will make the apparent failure turn into a smashing success.

One of my students had set a goal of a certain business deal that seemed highly desirable to him. He worked for many weeks to get the deal done. When the crucial time came, he failed miserably in a perfectly inexplicable way. It seemed as if the world had secretly conspired against him.

He chose not to be disappointed. In fact, he thanked God that his plan had been overruled, and he just continued forward with a grateful mind (don't forget that gratitude). In a few weeks, a deal came along that absolutely blew away the first deal. It was so good that it made the first deal look pale.

He saw that a mind which knew more than he knew had prevented him from missing out on the bigger deal by getting tangled up in the smaller one.

This is exactly how every seeming failure will work out for you. That is, of course, if you keep your faith, hold to your purpose, have gratitude; and do, every day, everything you can do, doing each separate act in a successful manner.

If you have what appears to be a failure, it is likely because you have not asked for enough. Keep moving forward, and something larger than what you had requested will find its way to you. Remember this. You will not fail because you messed up or because you don't have the necessary talent to do what you want to do. If you move forward as I have outlined, you will develop all the talent that is needed to do the job. It's not within the scope of this book to teach you the science of cultivating talent - just know it is as certain and simple as the science of attracting money.

However, don't hesitate or waver because you're afraid that you may fail due to lack of ability. Keep moving forward and when you get to the point of needing it, the ability will show up. The same source of ability which enabled an untrained Abraham Lincoln to do some of the greatest work in government ever accomplished by a single person is available to you. You can draw on all the wisdom and knowledge there is to meet the challenges that face you.

Move forward in full faith. Study this book. Have it readily available on your tablet or reader. Look at it frequently until you've mastered all the ideas in it. While you are firmly establishing your faith, you would be well served to minimize recreation and pleasure that may distract you from your goals. Stay away from people and places where conflicting ideas may be taught or spoken (such as well-intentioned friends who claim to know better than you but who are broke).

Don't read pessimistic material. Don't get into arguments about this stuff with others who refuse to consider the possibilities.

Spend most of your spare time contemplating your vision, cultivating gratitude, and re-reading this material. Everything you need to know about the science of attracting money is in this book.

We'll tie it up in a nice, neat package and put a ribbon on it, in the next and final chapter.

Chapter 17
Summary and Conclusion

"Now this is not the end. It is not even the beginning of the end. But it is, perhaps, the end of the beginning."

(Sir Winston Churchill, British political leader, 1874 -1965)

As we near the end of our journey together, I'll lay out our final, detailed thesis statement:

There is a thinking stuff from which all things are made and which, in its original state, permeates, penetrates, and fills every nook and cranny of the universe. A thought, held in this substance, produces the thing that is imaged by the thought. You can form things in your thought and, by impressing your thought upon formless substance (aka the universe), you can cause the thing you think about to be created.

In order to do this, you must pass from the competitive to the creative mind; otherwise you cannot be in harmony with the universe, which is always creative and never competitive in spirit.

To be in full harmony with the universe, you must enthusiastically express profound gratitude for what you have already received. This causes your mind to be unified with the intelligence of the universe, so that the universe can receive your thoughts. For you to stay on the creative plane, you must stay in harmony with the universe through a deep and continuous feeling of gratitude.

You must form a clear and definite mental image of what you want to have, to do, or to become. You must hold this mental image in your thoughts, while being deeply grateful to the Supreme that all your desires are granted to you. If you want to attract money, you should spend a fair amount of your free time fixed on your vision while, at the same time, giving sincere thanks that the reality of that vision is being given to you.

It is impossible to overstate the importance of frequent contemplation of the vision, coupled with unwavering faith and devout gratitude. This is the only way to guarantee that the universe will receive the image and that the creative forces to deliver it will be set in motion.

Once those forces are set in motion, the creative energy will work through established channels to deliver on the image. Everything that is clearly included in the image that is transmitted to the universe will come back in physical form to you, if and only if you follow these instructions to the letter and your faith does not waver.

The thing that you desire will generally be delivered through established business channels. In order to receive what you have wished, you must be active. This activity comes by more than filling your present "place."

You must always remember your intention to attract money and the things it buys through the realization of your mental image. You must do, every day, all that can be done, and do each act successfully. You must always give a "use" value that is greater than the cash value of a deal. You must project the "impression of increase" to everyone you meet.

If you practice these rules to the letter, you will absolutely attract money and the things it buys; and the money you receive will be in direct proportion to the definiteness of your vision, the firmness of your purpose, the steadiness of your faith, and the depth of your gratitude.

And so we come to the end, although I hope you will consider it to be the beginning of a new way of acting, living, and receiving. Please study this material carefully, and use it wisely. Your successes may be small and subtle at first. As you focus on the process, your successes will grow and so will you.

Enjoy your coming prosperity, with profound gratitude.

Appendix
Let Me Show My "Profound Gratitude"

"Gratitude is the sign of noble souls."

(Aesop, Greek story teller, circa 620–564 BC)

As I've promised you throughout this book, if you follow this process exactly, it will work and it will work for you. You will begin attracting money, subtly at first and in more obvious ways as you go forward.

Every step of the process is critical. Leave one of them out and you will fail. Follow them all and you will succeed.

For me, one of the most difficult steps to master was the whole "gratitude" thing. I always wanted a bigger house, a fancier car, a fatter bank account. So how could it possibly make sense to be thankful for what I had, when I felt it was not nearly what I wanted? Isn't that the same as settling, being content, just not trying?

It took a while to grasp the "like attracts like" concept. If I wanted a nicer house, I learned to incorporate profound gratitude for the one I already had into my request. I learned to be deeply grateful for the good times that my family enjoyed at the smaller house, for the excellent job it did keeping us warm in the winter and comfortable in the summer, for the ease with which I could get to my barbecue grill because everything I had in the house was close by, and so on.

I realized that to complain about the small house was to focus on the things I *did not* like, thus attracting more of the same. Think hard about the process you've just learned. You don't get what you ask for - you get what you predominantly think about!

With your permission, I'll share how I got really good and really consistent about expressing profound gratitude. Remember that you can express your gratitude to a higher power, the universe, God, or to nobody in particular, depending on your personal beliefs - but you need to express it!

So with that in mind, here's how I remembered to do it regularly. I know, it sounds silly, but hear me out.

I have a small, very special but non-precious gemstone which I carry with me in my pocket at all times. Several times a day, whenever I think about it; I grab the stone, close my hand around it, and give thanks for good things I have enjoyed that day.

They may be a good meal, the company of my lovely wife, some money that came my way or even just beautiful weather.

If I'm in a public place, I do this fervently but silently, in a way that nobody else will know what I'm doing.

The same applies if I'm in private, such as in my car except, in that case, I express my gratitude vocally, loudly, and enthusiastically (though I don't let other drivers see what I'm up to).

Let me remind you that you need to not only be grateful for the things you have received, but for the fact that you *are* receiving (not *will* receive) the things you have asked for. I use the gratitude rock for my "asks" in the exact same way, "I am so happy and grateful that I am receiving (whatever it is I've asked for)."

I hope this doesn't sound too crazy. It's not about the special gemstone itself (even though I've personally picked it out and given gratitude with it). It's about using a method to channel and amplify your gratitude on a regular basis, with feeling.

This works for me, and if you'll use it in conjunction with the other parts of the process, it will work for you. To show my gratitude to as many of the readers of this book as possible, I've arranged to give away free Gratitude Gemstones to the first 1,000 people who ask for them (you just pay for shipping and handling).

Let's be clear: Profound gratitude is an absolutely critical part of this process. The Gratitude Gemstone is my gift to you, to help you easily remember to express profound gratitude! If you let it, the Gratitude Gemstone will make this part of the process easier and more consistent for you.

I urge you to claim yours today.

Get Your Free Gratitude Gemstone

To get your free Gratitude Gemstone while the supply lasts, simply go now to: www.lifes-not-rocket-science.com/gratitude.htm and we'll have it to you in no time.

Thanks again—I hope you've enjoyed this book as much as I've enjoyed bringing it to you.

If you liked this book, please follow us on Facebook https://www.facebook.com/pages/Lifes-Not-Rocket-Science/174764252684756 for uplifting quotes of the day, little tidbits of wisdom, and the announcement of our next book.